Contents

THE CHRISTMAN FILE

The Christman File

W. J. CHRISTMAN

THE SAINT ANDREW PRESS
EDINBURGH

First published in 1978 by
THE SAINT ANDREW PRESS
121 George Street, Edinburgh

© W. J. CHRISTMAN 1978

ISBN 0 7152 0400 9

Printed in Great Britain by
Thomson Litho Ltd., East Kilbride, Scotland.
Bound by Hunter & Foulis, Edinburgh.

CHAPTER ONE

The Call

The bus conductor had his little laugh at my American accent when I asked him to tell me the location of Richmond Craigmillar church.

'There are two churches on Niddrie Mains Road. You can take your pick'.

I snuggled down into my overcoat and peered out into the darkness. The weather in January 1965 was no better than in any other year. The wind was carrying torrents of freezing rain straight into the heart of the bus.

One of the passengers told me that we had arrived in Niddrie. Reluctantly, I left the shelter of the bus and sought the only building where distant lights gave a promise of warmth and companionship. It turned out to be Richmond Craigmillar church. I had made my journey in order to address the Sunday evening youth fellowship. Already I wished that I was home.

Home for me was the New College residence. I had lived there for five years—first as a divinity student and later as Assistant to the Professor of Ecclesiastical History. As a student, I had been assured by students and staff alike that I would never be able to take the degree. 'All Yanks are fools' had been a common proverb. However, by dogged determination rather than intellectual brilliance I had managed to do it. I was not particularly happy in my present vocation. The art of lecturing seemed to elude me. It was a matter of finding the right language and I had not yet found it. Since there was no community structure within the New College, I did not know whom I was addressing. Lacking an identity—without a sense of belonging to any group—I longed to return to the United States.

The address to the youth fellowship went well. As a result, a number of the boys and girls from the fellowship accepted my invitation to come for coffee to the residence later in the week. While they were with me, the telephone rang. It was Colin Anderson, Assistant Minister of Liberton Kirk, and a former student of mine. He knew that I had considered returning to America and that I was restless in the academic world. His minister was interim moderator for the vacant charge of Richmond Craigmillar. Since I was due to preach at Liberton Kirk in one week's time, would I allow its vacancy committee to come along and listen to me? I agreed without much reflection. It occurred to me that any one could come along to hear me preach, regardless of my own attitude to his presence.

A few days passed and I led the worship service at Liberton Kirk. After the service, the Church Officer told me that a number of people wished to see me in the vestry. I assumed that these were the usual number of well-wishers from the congregation. I was surprised, therefore, to find myself meeting together with the vacancy committee of Richmond Craigmillar. I had forgotten all about them!

The interview was somewhat amusing. The

2

committee assumed that I wished to be their new minister. Initially, I had no such intention. However, as our discussion progressed my attitude changed. The committee told a tale about a difficult community and a lively congregation. The members explained that the nature of the district had discouraged prospective candidates. They described the post as 'a challenge'. Later I was to learn that all vacancy committee's make use of this type of language. However, by the end of our conversation, I had become so impressed by the approach which had been made to me that I undertook to consider the matter carefully and to inform the committee about my eventual decision in one month's time.

As I considered what course to follow, I asked for advice from my friends. Most were emphatic. I should never consider leaving academic life for the life of the parish, and especially not for this particular parish. Richmond Craigmillar was a church struggling to keep alive. Its lack of success was reflected in the figures given in the current Church of Scotland Yearbook for 1965. On paper its membership numbered about 850. Yet its annual giving was in the region of £1,500. Obviously, this was not 'a lively congregation'. Unaided, it could never have called a minister in the first place. Yet the church also had the services of an assistant minister and a deaconess; both of whose salaries were paid by the Church of Scotland Home Board. I had known similar cases of 'feather-bedding' in regard to country churches but this was the first time that I had made the acquaintance of a city congregation which owed its very existence to the generosity of other churches. It seemed quite apparent that, although the area might be a difficult one, the congregation of Richmond Craigmillar was in dire straits itself.

'It is never a failure to be a failure at Richmond Craigmillar'. With these wise words, Professor Cheyne, my immediate superior, urged that I seek a charge elsewhere. He was not the only man to give me this kind of advice. Most experienced men in the parish ministry agreed that it would be far wiser for a beginner to look for a charge in the country-side. Once I had grasped the rudiments of congregational life, I would be better equipped to cope with the demands of a parish like Craigmillar. I knew that they were right. Had the situation been different, I should have followed their advice and accepted their wisdom without question. But this was a situation which addressed a question directly to me. I was being asked to accept the leadership of a disheartened congregation in the midst of a disastrous area with no reasonable hope of ever being able to alter the condition of either the church or the community. I had not sought this challenge. It had found me.

The only way to find an answer was by prayer. My previous experience had not prepared me for the parish ministry. In nine months as a student assistant in 1961, I had not attended a single meeting of the Kirk Session. I had no knowledge of the nature of the Congregational Board except what I could glean from a reading of church law. One look at the manse filled me with dismay. A single man, I had no notion as to how to bring the domestic touch to a seven-room house with a large garden. I had no knowledge of the mechanism of the welfare state, and I knew that many of the residents of Richmond Craigmillar parish were dependant upon it for their existence. The fact that no other minister of the Church of Scotland had been willing to accept the vacancy indicated that I would be foolish indeed to go there.

Perhaps it was just this awareness of ignorance on my part which uncovered a stubborn streak in me. Perhaps it was the desperate situation of the congregation which forced me to take its challenge seriously. I was young and I had energy. I knew that at the very least I could climb the stairs to visit the sick and the lonely. Although my American accent always inspired ridicule on the part of the young I had, through previous experience, mastered the vernacular of the tenements and the closes. But there was more. I came to the conclusion that if it was God's will that I should accept this call, then no other consideration should possibly compel me to reject it. I prayed. And, out of searching and dedication and through an experience of the love of God, came the charge to accept the challenge which had been thrust upon me. My decision was that I should heed the call.

Months flew by. The General Assembly accepted me as a minister of the Church of Scotland since previously I had been ordained in the United Presbyterian Church in America. Eventually, it was all over. Or rather, it had all begun.

On July 21, 1965 I was inducted to the vacant charge of Richmond Craigmillar parish church. In the next issue of *The British Weekly* there appeared a letter written by an 'Indignant Minister's Wife'. The letter complained that an Edinburgh charge should have been given to an American:

'My astonishment is caused by the disclosure at the General Assembly and in *Life and Work* at the beginning of last year that many probationers, men brought up and trained in our own church and colleges, find themselves without parishes. Surely the General Assembly should consider the members of our own church first before admitting people from other denominations. . . .'

CHAPTER TWO

The Face of my Parish

At the beginning of the nineteenth century, the district adjacent to Craigmillar Castle, south of Edinburgh, was an odd mixture of agricultural and industrial elements. The Reverend James Begg, in his account of his parish, mentions 'an excellent and valuable sandstone quarry at Niddry' and the presence of 'a new steam thrashing mill' in the same village. At the same time, Begg takes note of the gardens and the hedges (thirty feet high in one instance) in the same vicinity and counts 'about two hundred fowl, poultry, geese, turkeys'. (in *The New Statistical Account of Scotland*, I, pp. 16f, 1845)

Several years later, Hugh Milier, a future spokesman for the Free Church of Scotland, was employed as a stone mason in the same district. He describes Niddry village in the following manner:

'One of these (collier) villages, whose foundations can no longer be traced, occurred in the immediate vicinity of Niddry Mill. It was a wretched assemblage of dingy, low-roofed, tile-covered hovels, each of which perfectly resembled all the others, and was inhabited by a rude and ignorant race of men, that still bore about them the soil and stain of recent slavery.' (*My Schools and Schoolmasters*, p.314, 1905).

Miller distinguishes four types of labourers who compose the village population. Most of these, he says, are old people, farm servants in the decline of life. There are also colliers; and there are carters who make their living by carrying materials from the Niddry quarry into the city. Finally, there are the mechanics who are employed in the coal pits. Miller contrasts the lot of these grim products of the industrial revolution with that of the local landowner. He mentions the estate of one John Wauchope and tells of his own delight in 'the shade of the Niddry woods'.

'Though shut out, however, from the neighbouring fields and policies, the Niddry woods were open to me; and I have enjoyed many an agreeable saunter along a broad, planted belt; with a grassy path in the midst, that form the southern boundary, and through whose long vista I could see the sun sink over the picturesque ruins of Craigmillar Castle'. (*op. cit.*, p.31a)

One hundred years later, the fields of the Wauchope Estates, forbidden to the stone mason, were being turned into paved streets and the Niddrie Quarry had given its name to one of Edinburgh's first housing estates: Niddrie Mains.

In 1934, the Edinburgh Corporation built housing estates at Craigmillar and at Niddrie Mains. Two thousand, five hundred and ninety-three houses were built. Roughly one-third of these was located close to Craigmillar Castle. The remainder was situated at Niddrie Mains. In both of these estates, there was an average of twenty-four houses built per acre of land. The resultant level of density was high, one hundred persons per acre. Most of the families who moved into these new houses had been transported as a result of the Slum Clearance Programme under way in Edinburgh's Canongate district. Overcrowding was nothing new to these people. The majority had lived in two-apartment or three-apartment houses. They paid a very low rent for these Canongate houses which were in a deplorable condition:

'In one (Canongate) family, two parents with two sons aged 16 and 6 and three daughters aged 12, 11 and 3 lived in two rooms. In another family, where a mother, two sons and two daughters all over 17, occupied two rooms, the mother alone was able to sleep in the living-room as only one corner was free enough from damp to allow a bed to be placed; so the four children had to sleep in three beds in the small bedroom. In yet another family, the father, mother and small son slept in one bed, while the daughter aged 16 and son aged 13 slept in another'. (David Keir, Ed., *The Third Statistical Account of Scotland*, pp.35f., 1966)

In 1935, the Housing (Scotland) Act was published. This was a major enactment which, for the first time, fixed a national minimum standard for measuring overcrowding. The standard itself was not very high. It allowed the sitting-room to be used for sleeping, counted children under the age of ten as only half-persons and ignored the existence of babies altogether. Nevertheless, its effect was to make a great improvement on the conditions which had existed previously. The duty was laid on the local authorities to survey their areas and to submit

9

proposals for building the houses needed to end overcrowding. If there was a failure to adhere to the stipulations of the Act, the result might be the forfeiture of the Central Government's Housing Subsidies.

The result was dramatic. In order to alleviate over-crowding, housing estates were erected at Niddrie Mains, Craigmillar and Pilton in the City of Edinburgh. These houses were built closely together. Other than the Pilton Estate built at roughly the same time, only the two schemes at Niddrie Mains and Craigmillar had such a high density in the whole of Edinburgh. However, the people from the Canongate were probably little troubled by the close proximity of their neighbours. They moved willingly into the three- and four-apartment houses within the new estates. Typically, six of these houses would be grouped together around a single stair in a building with three floors.

Shortly after the Second World War, further housing extensions were carried out in the Niddrie Marischal and Bingham districts. Finally, the housing estates at Niddrie Mill, Greendykes and Magdalene were completed during the 1950's. Altogether, therefore, the Craigmillar Ward in 1965 contained the following housing schemes:

Niddrie Mains	Niddrie Mill
Niddrie Marischal	Bingham
Craigmillar	Magdalene
Greendykes	

Although there were a few private homes within the Ward, the vast majority of houses had been built by the Edinburgh Corporation.

The total population of the Craigmillar Ward at this time was in the region of seventeen thousand. According to statistics compiled in 1965 by the Edinburgh Council of Social Service, Craigmillar was the worst Edinburgh Ward for juvenile delinquency, children taken into care by the Corporation, overcrowding and pulmonary tuberculosis. It was the second worst Ward for attempted suicides, evictions, disturbances of the peace and infant mortality. It was the fourth worst for school truancy and still-births. Altogether, the people of the new Craigmillar Ward appear to have suffered from a greater social disability than had ever been their lot within the narrow confines of the Canongate. With the best of intentions, the Edinburgh Corporation appeared to have manufactured another slum.

Richmond Craigmillar parish included two of the older housing estates built within the Craigmillar Ward: Niddrie Mains and Niddrie Marischal. Niddrie Mains Road divided the two estates from one another and there was a sense of distinction between the populations of each district. As a matter of fact, each of the estates which comprised the Craigmillar Ward felt itself to be separate and apart from its neighbours, a point made by Mr Jack Nixon, a youth worker employed in the parish between 1963 and 1965:

'Almost all my work was being done in the central part of the Niddrie scheme and it was easily the toughest and most aggressive part of the whole area. I should say at this point that the area Niddrie/Craigmillar is quite definitely split into four distinctive areas each with its separate code.

I should also confess that originally the Mag-
dalenes and the Binghams were in my area but I
have never seriously been involved in these
schemes. The Railway Line divides Niddrie from
the Binghams and is therefore apart.' (*Experiment with 'Unattached' in Niddrie/Craigmillar*,
p.2)

In 1965 there were approximately eight thousand
people living in the parish. At this time, these people
were served by the following shopping facilities:

Grocers' shops (7)
General stores (2)
Butcher's shop (1)
Post Offices (2)
Chemist's Shop (2)
Fish and Chip Bars (3)
Launderettes (2)
Used Furniture Shop (1)

Social and recreational facilities were not abundant either:

Elementary Schools (2)
Secondary Schools (1)
Churches (5: Church of Scotland, Free Church,
    Roman Catholic Church, Scottish Episcopal
    Church, Salvation Army)
Adventure Playground (1)
Community Centre (1)
Children's Play Centre (1)
Bingo Hall (1)
Licensed Betting Shop (2)
Social Club (1)

There were no public houses within the parish

because of a clause which Lady Wauchope had inserted into the Bill of Sale for her lands forbidding the presence of such establishments. The parish was served by two buses. A trip to the city centre took approximately twenty minutes.

Richmond Craigmillar parish church had originally been the parish church of North Richmond Street in the City of Edinburgh. Founded in 1845, the church continued at that location until 1933. In that year, the Edinburgh Corporation purchased the site of the church for redevelopment, paying the congregation £6,000 plus a free site for the new church. As many parishioners were now moving to the new Niddrie Mains housing estate, the church followed the people and a new location for the congregation was found in Niddrie Mains Road. On September 18, 1935, the new buildings—costing £10,000—were dedicated by the then Moderator of the General Assembly.

Thirty years later in 1965, I was called to be the minister of Richmond Craigmillar parish church. Its walls, constructed of Craigmillar stone, were black with soot; its grounds littered with empty beer cans. A few of its windows had been broken, the rest were screened from further damage by wire mesh. The church shared its air of dereliction with its parish. By day, sunlight fell upon unattended gardens, shattered glass and broken fences. Overflowing dustbins and a variety of refuse littered the streets, whose only ornaments were the glittering fragments of broken bottles. The grey faces of concrete houses succeeded one another until the eye lost count. At night there was almost total darkness. Street lamps seemed to burn at only half their normal voltage.

Light bulbs had long since been snatched from the closes, leaving only gaping sockets. Evening mists concealed a variety of activities: men on the roof-tops breaking-in to the homes below, women rushing along the streets whimpering quietly to themselves, children writing obscenities on doorways, dogs urinating in the passages and the constant and fretful procession of wandering, willful teenagers. It was difficult to know which to prefer in my new parish: day or night, wakefulness or forgetfulness.

CHAPTER THREE

Enter Douglas Templeton

I had been called to become the minister of Richmond Craigmillar parish church. Others had been called to serve there as well. Ena Finlayson, the deaconess, had continued to work in the church throughout the entire vacancy. I had met her previously when speaking to the youth fellowship. At first glance, she appeared to be a tiny, fragile little creature. She was quietly-spoken and her gestures conveyed an impression of calmness and humility. First impressions of Ena, however, were a bit misleading. Her dedication to God had summoned her away from her job as a bank clerkess in Hawick, carried her through the years of her training, and at last had called her to serve as deaconess at Richmond Craigmillar. All of this indicated a will of iron, and that will was in evidence from time to time during the years in which we worked together. Yet it was a will which was entirely subordinate to the task of serving her Lord and Saviour.

The other indispensable member of our 'team' was the church officer, David Gunn. He had served with the two previous ministers in the church. Now a man in his sixties, he was well versed in the art of aiding the minister. The deficiencies of the church building, the details of the numerous organisations and the mechanism of the morning worship service were all matters which David had mastered years before.

Between them, these two people piloted me through the difficult months of my early ministry. At the beginning, I was faced with a variety of official documents—mostly concerning baptism or weddings—which quite bewildered me. Ena took me in hand. She efficiently translated the official jargon of the Church of Scotland into intelligible English. I looked upon her with more awe than I had felt for my Professor of Hebrew! Organisations also were a mystery to me. Although I had previously been acquainted with the Boy Scout movement, I had no conceivable notion as to what the Boys' Brigade or the Girl Guides did to while away their hours. The Guild of Friendship sounded like a Quaker group to me; it turned out to be a band of elderly women. And, although I was aware that the Woman's Guild had a national reputation as being a formidable group of ladies, I did not possess any information regarding its administrative structure. David Gunn explained the inner workings of these various organisations in his down-to-earth way. Although he was an elderly man and failing in his health, he came along day after day to the church to help in any way that he was needed. A baker, he could often be seen at four or five in the morning, waiting to catch the bus for work. Yet by tea-time, and sometimes before, he could also be seen mending the door of the church hall, washing the walls of the Kirk, or judging which organisation had the better right to use the hall. As a result of the training which I received from these two, I took my first steps, like a toddler, in the ministry of the Church of Scotland.

The most necessary member of the 'team', however, had yet to be discovered. The church had been without an assistant minister for over a year. By the time that I arrived on the scene, the supply of graduating divinity students had been exhausted. They had all gone to become assistants in other churches. However, a grant from the Home Board of the Church of Scotland existed to provide the salary of an assistant minister for Richmond Craigmillar. I was determined to find one. In such a large and difficult parish, it was obvious that we were going to need all the help that we could get. In the event, however, finding an assistant proved an impossible task. The few men who might have been free to take up the appointment were appalled at the prospect of working in Niddrie. Although it might have been possible to find an American who would have been willing to work for a single year, I was certain that it was necessary to locate a Scot for the task. One foreigner was enough for Niddrie for the moment! My only chance, therefore, was to attract a qualified man back into the Christian ministry. The Church of Scotland *Yearbook* listed a number of probationers who, for one reason or another, had decided to teach or to work in industry. By writing letters and by making ample use of the telephone, I arranged a number of interviews with these men. Although I met many interesting personalities during the course of my search, I failed to attract any one to the task of serving as assistant minister at Richmond Craigmillar.

One morning, however, the telephone rang. It

was Jim Blackie, Professor of Practical Theology at the New College. He told me that there was a fellow named Douglas Templeton who had been working for his doctorate at Tübingen in Germany. Although he lacked any experience of parish work, he did qualify as a probationer of the Church of Scotland. Professor Blackie thought that he might be willing to serve as my assistant if I could persuade him that the job would be interesting. I was a bit apprehensive. After enquiry, I learned that Douglas was some years older than myself. Would an older man be willing to serve with a younger fellow, especially one so inexperienced as myself? Furthermore, there was the question of his theology. It was hinted darkly that he was 'far out', a liberal, and that 'he didn't know what he believed'. Although I had no practical experience of parish work, it seemed to me that the last thing we needed at Richmond Craigmillar was an academic who would ponder theological complexities while more down-to-earth work needed to be done. However, I decided that it would do no harm to meet the man, and an interview was arranged through the kind offices of Professor Blackie. I agreed to meet Douglas Templeton at the University of Edinburgh Staff Club.

I arrived at the club shortly before the appointed hour of 4 p.m. wearing a clerical collar and a black suit. I was more or less certain that this was an appropriate attire for an interview with a fellow clergyman. I was also under the impression that the outfit might help to identify me more readily as the Richmond Craigmillar man-of-the-cloth. I sat for five minutes on a comfortable seat in the lounge reflecting upon the fact that my academic life was over and that my membership in the staff club would very shortly expire. No-one entered the room during this time. Looking around, I could see three men— all fat, balding and red-faced. By the wildest stretch of the imagination, I could not think that any of these could possibly qualify as prospective assistants for my church. The minutes ticked by. No-one appeared. At last, I went outside to have a look around. It was a brilliant day, complete with genuine sunshine and blue sky. But there was no-one who looked like an assistant minister. I stood and waited. Slowly, I became aware of a figure eyeing me on my left. When I looked around, my instinctive reaction was defensive. I had met this type of fellow before: long brown hair hanging well over his ears and face, brown skin which was probably due more to dirt than sunshine, an old corduroy jacket and a loosely-fitting pair of trousers. Inwardly, I cursed my resemblance to a 'G.I. Joe'. Undoubtedly this fellow wanted a hand-out, half-a-crown for a meal which he would spend on drink. I decided to get my money's worth for once, however, and to ask him a question: 'Could you tell me if a Minister has passed by recently?'

The man stretched out his hand, 'Mr Christman?' he asked, 'My name is Douglas Templeton'.

Douglas Templeton was not odd, but he was not commonplace either. In our first interview, I was of the opinion that here was a man of perceptive mind and an open and friendly nature. The 'dirt' wasn't dirt either, but the result of many weeks spent mountain-climbing in the Alps. I put my cards on the table. I told Douglas just how ignorant I was about the ways and means of the Church of Scotland. For this reason, I hoped that we might be able to work together as a team rather than in a minister-assistant relationship. I had prepared an outline of the type of work with which he could be involved at Richmond Craigmillar. It included Bible classes and Sunday schools, pastoral visitations and hospital afternoons. As we talked, I determined to keep the outline in my pocket. Douglas was not at all interested in the more traditional forms of the parish ministry. Relationships with people, and with groups of people, concerned him a great deal more. In general, we sketched out the direction that we would follow together. I would function as the more traditional ecclesiastical figure, a role for which I was not particularly 'type-cast'; Douglas would explore the group-structures which existed within the parish. I was to work within the church; he was to work on the outside. I had no idea as to whether this procedure would prove beneficial to Richmond Craigmillar. Since I was so poorly equipped, by background and experience, for the job which I had undertaken, I was in no position to make a competent judgment. Yet here was a man who at least was willing to come and to serve in Niddrie. As we parted company, it occurred to me that any man was better than no assistant at all.

The next problem was to find Douglas a suitable base for his parish explorations. We agreed that ideally this would take the form of lodgings. Living with a member of the congregation might have been inhibiting to his work or provoked jealousy within the church. So we decided to look for 'digs' in a home which had no connection with the congregation but which was located centrally within the parish. One day I was having lunch in a little restaurant in the High Street. Chatting with the waitress, I happened to mention that I was the new minister at Richmond Craigmillar.

'Oh yes' she replied, 'I go by there often on the way to bingo'.

Local residents were the best patrons of the Niddrie Bingo, which they had christened 'The Gaff', so I asked the waitress if she would ask her fellow bingo-players about the possibility of lodgings for Douglas. Since the Jehovah's Witnesses had already lodged several members of their convention in Niddrie a few years before, a suitable precedent had already been created! The waitress did as she was asked and came back with the information that a certain Mrs Forbes of Niddrie Mains Terrace would consider giving accommodation to Douglas.

In the person of Kate Forbes, we acquired another important member of our unofficial 'team'. Mrs Forbes was a widow who had lived in Niddrie for a number of years. Her close was situated in the heart of what was generally described as the most difficult street in the district. It was peopled by characters of dubious conduct. The gardens were untended and there was often a pile of rubbish standing in the street outside. Several of the houses had been fumigated time and time again by the Cleansing Department without any obvious effect on their inhabitants. Small children hung out of the windows like models for a Giles' cartoon, while the dogs alternately wooed and fought one another in the darkened close. In the midst of such an environment, Mrs Forbes demonstrated cleanliness and a certain amount of godliness. Her home was always spotless and tidy. Her manner was frank and open.

If she did not like any one, she said so—and often it appeared that 'any one' was 'every one'. But life had been hard to Kate Forbes and left her with little patience for soft ways. She would never join the Church, she said, and she enjoyed her game of bingo. Yet, when she thought that no-one was looking, her good heart gave her away. Often she was the first person in the stair to help those whom she judged to be genuinely in need of help.

Although Mrs Forbes was suspicious about the prospect of taking Douglas into her house, she agreed to meet him. One night, there was a knock at her door. The good widow put down her hand of cards and left her friend in order to answer it. Outside stood the unique Douglas.

'I'm Dougie', he said, 'I've come to stay'.

Then he deposited a great pile of books at her feet and leaped down the steps to bring up more. The lady gasped with surprise. Surely, this could be no minister; he seemed like such an ordinary fellow! But appearances had proved deceptive to Mrs Forbes. For the next two years of his residence in Niddrie Mains Terrace, 'ordinary' Douglas kept his landlady gasping. He had made his first conquest. And our 'team' was complete at last.

CHAPTER FOUR

The Question of Baptism

'What are you going to do about baptisms?'

The question came from the church elder who was the only member of the Kirk Session to have persevered with the interior decoration of the manse. The other members of the congregation were either on holiday or had forgotten their original promises to help him. It was August, but a cold wind blew through the empty rooms. I had assembled a bed, a desk and a housekeeper who had affirmed her intention to cook and clean for a salary of three pounds per week. (It *was* 1965!).

It had not occurred to me that I needed to do anything in particular about baptisms. It seemed reasonable that they should occur from time to time, like the weather or a common cold. I supposed that a minister need only to cling to *The Book of Common Order* and somehow muddle through. According to the elder, however, the procedure was more complex than I had reckoned. I would need to take each baby in my arms! This had been the practice of my predecessor and, I was told, it made 'a pretty picture'. The picture in my own mind was somewhat different, however. I had once witnessed a baptism service in which the minister nearly dropped one of the babies into the centre of a deep and well-filled

23

baptismal font. I wondered if it would be possible to take out an insurance policy against such risks.

It soon became apparent, however, that the elder's question concealed a problem of a more complex nature. This was evident at the first meeting of the Kirk Session. Several years prior to my induction, the General Assembly of the Church of Scotland had formulated a series of instructions concerning the act of baptism. It had stated then that one or both parents of the child should be communicant members of the church. There was one rather vague statement that the Kirk Session might be prepared to shepherd the parents into membership. Otherwise, the instructions were quite straight-forward and unequivocal.

During the vacancy, the locum minister had been obedient to these rules and had refused to baptise when neither parent was a church member. This had created a certain amount of ill feeling within the parish. Previously, ministers of Richmond Craigmillar, uninhibited by the new Assembly regulations, had baptised all the bairns brought forward for their blessing. People continued to expect the parish minister to do this. Undoubtedly in their eyes 'doing the bairn' had nothing to do with faith or the church. It was simply an act which brought good luck and an excuse for a party. But the rules had changed. Now parents were required to join the church and to attend communicants' classes prior to the act of baptism. Several had followed this procedure. Once their babies had been baptised, however, they were never seen again! The church records indicated that they had not even bothered to attend their first communion.

This, then, was the problem: to baptise or not to baptise. And, if to baptise, on what conditions? To follow the rules was the simple solution. However, it appeared that in Niddrie the rules were not producing the appropriate results. They were alienating rather than attracting people to the church. I was singularly unequipped to deal with the matter. Previous to our Session discussion, I had not even realised that there was a problem. For this reason, I turned to the elders for advice on the matter. After a good deal of consideration, the Session decided to follow the lead of the Session Clerk, a man who had lived in Niddrie for many years and who had devoted his life to the service of its church. It was decided that rather than compel the parents to join the church, we should instead encourage them to do so. However, the door to baptism would remain closed to the children of parents living outside the parish unless they were members of Richmond Craigmillar.

I now had two sets of instructions to guide me: one from the General Assembly and one from the Kirk Session. When in doubt, I decided to depend upon the wisdom of the elders, all local men who knew our specific situation quite well. Upon reflection, it occurred to me that in reality we were making use of the sacrament of baptism for a missionary purpose, hoping to draw parents into the circumference of the church without compelling them initially into an either-or confrontation. I accepted the advice of the elders. Only later was I to realise how greatly this single decision had shaped the direction of my entire ministry at Richmond Craigmillar.

Vestry nights were held on Wednesday evenings. Officially, the minister was in his office for consultation between the hours of seven and eight p.m. More typically, however, it was long past the hour of nine before I left the church on vestry nights. These evenings were beyond belief. When I arrived, I might find as many as forty people, all seated and waiting for a conference with me. It was, for many, the only opportunity that they might have for a contact with 'a Professional' during evening hours. The teachers, social workers and health visitors in the district had all finished their work and gone home. Leaving me. This explained the wide variety of problems represented at the vestry night.

My first look at them frightened me thoroughly. Eager young couples sat shoulder to shoulder with alcoholics and ex-convicts. All had come for a reason: they wanted something from the church. What they could not get from the church, they expected to get from me. The young couples had come along to get married. Their banns would be read out at the morning worship service and most would decide to be married in Richmond Craigmillar. The alcoholics and ex-prisoners had mostly come along to 'try me on', to ask for money. More by instinct than by insight, I early hit upon a policy of 'No Money'. Food, and sometimes clothing, might be provided to families who, for one reason or another, were genuinely needy. Those who had come along, however, in hopes of shillings or pounds were directed to the office of the National Assistance. Initially, every request for help had to be investigated thoroughly. Over the years, however, many dependant families became well known to me.

So did the local 'con men'.

'Minister', said one fellow at the end of a vestry night, 'Me and my mate need the price of bus fare to North Berwick and back. We've got the chance of a job there'. Virtue and integrity were apparent in his face.

'That's all right, men,' said I, 'I have to make a call in that direction. I'll take you myself'.

'Oh, but Minister, we wouldn't want to take you out of your way', the man protested.

But I was going in that precise direction. Reluctantly, the two men climbed into my car. Thirty minutes later I let them out in North Berwick. They didn't say a word. On the way back to Niddrie, I congratulated myself on giving two fellows a helping hand. One week afterwards, however, a young lad told me that he had seen two middle-aged men walking into Niddrie from the direction of North Berwick and cursing me all the while. He thought that it was most peculiar—and so did I, until I remembered that the return fare to North Berwick would have bought each man three pints of beer!

Some people, old as well as young, had come along to the vestry in order to obtain a character-reference from me. It did not matter that I had never met them previously. I was expected to write them a character-reference in order to help them gain future employment. I learned to be careful with such people. On one of my early vestry nights, a young fellow in his early twenties came along to ask for one. I had seen him at the Morning worship service and, since he had taken the time to come to church, I took the time to write him a glowing reference testifying to his church attendance and to his honesty. Two days later, I received a visit from the police. In response to the policeman's question, I replied that I had indeed written a character-reference for the young man. The policeman scolded me gently. That morning, the lad in question had been found guilty of forty-two charges of petty larceny. In defence, he had produced my reference!

Occasionally, an hysterical woman would make an appearance at the vestry night. She would have come to create amateur dramatics with the new minister. I had encounters with two such females on my first vestry evening and was thoroughly shaken as a result. Having studied church history, I was aware that Saint Augustine (a bachelor like myself) had always insisted upon the presence of a fellow-clergyman when interviewing ladies in his vestry. I decided to do the next best thing and asked for the presence of Miss Finlayson, ostensibly to help as a secretary but really for moral support in the midst of turbulent emotional gales. Her presence had the desired effect of quieting hysterical passions. The ladies, however, deprived of their opportunity for emotional release, complained to their neighbours. In the end—at the suggestion of the Session Clerk—I had to do without Ena's help. But I stationed Davey Gunn just down the passageway in case I needed his glowering presence to restore order.

However, about one-half of the people who waited so patiently for a conference with me were parents seeking baptism for their children. Most were not members of any church. They had come along to ask for the baptism of their children for the following reasons:

1. They had themselves been baptised and married in the church. They held themselves to be Protestants. They now demanded that their children 'be done' as well.

2. They were lapsed Roman Catholics and believed that their children would suffer in Limbo should they die unbaptised. Afraid to go to a priest lest he should impose the discipline of the Catholic Church upon them, they turned to the Kirk to baptise their babies.

3. They wanted an excuse for a party.

4. A relation or friend had given their child a robe for the sacrament of baptism. If the baby went unbaptised for long, it would out-grow the garment.

Interviews with these people demanded a lot of time and effort. Since, in most cases, only the mother appeared with her unbaptised offspring, it was necessary to make a visit to the home in order to meet the recalcitrant father. I would begin our interview with a statement of the vows which both parents would be expected to take prior to the act of baptism. Basically, these were promises of faith in Jesus Christ and decisions to bring up the child in the teaching of the church. Could they take these vows without becoming hypocrites in the eyes of the congregation? Or in the eyes of God? Most young parents readily professed their belief in God and in Jesus Christ. They also freely admitted that they did not possess the knowledge necessary to educate their children in the teachings of the church. However, when it was pointed out to them that the communicants' classes might equip them with that knowledge, they demurred. It was not that they had anything against the church, they said, but they lacked the time to attend the morning worship service. Most were honest enough to admit that they could never attend these services except occasionally. They gave many reasons for this. Many seemed perfectly valid. In order to obtain a corporation house in Edinburgh, it was necessary for a young couple to have produced at least one child. The more babies in the family, the greater priority they were given for a house. These young children, however, kept the mother confined to the home. The father, on the other hand, was often compelled to work shifts or to apply for over-time in order to make a living wage for the support of his expanding family. The more responsible a fellow he was, the harder he worked. He hoped, by saving, to be able eventually to take his family out of Niddrie altogether and into a community of a more respectable nature. In general, the pattern of family life within the parish seemed to work against the possibility of regular church attendance by any believers except the very young or the very old.

Most of these interviews moved me deeply. In the end, I agreed to baptise the children of families resident within the parish, providing one or both parents would undertake to attempt to come to the next communicants' class. I did not force them to promise to come. I only said that they would be given notification of the date and time for the first class. In fairness, the great majority of these families did decide to join the church. Once they had become members, however, they were unlikely to be in their seats on a Sunday morning. Circumstances had conspired to prevent this from happening.

On the other hand, what was I to do when a parent refused point-blank to even consider becoming a member of the church? During my second vestry night, a woman came to ask for the baptism of her infant son. Her husband was a Protestant, she said. He would never join the church but he did support Rangers Football Club! She herself had once been a devout Catholic but she had lapsed from her faith at the time of her marriage. This was her first child and she wanted him to be baptised. I suggested that she should go across the road and ask for the priest. She was afraid to do this, however, because of her husband's anger. That being the case, I suggested that I would go along and interview her husband since he was the Protestant in the household. One or both of them would need to consider joining the church. The woman was in despair. She knew that her husband would never join, she said, but she did not feel that she could ever become a Protestant herself. Her roots in the Catholic Church were too deep. What was she to do? She believed that if her baby went unbaptised, then God's judgment would fall upon him. If he died, she said, he might burn in hell. In vain did I assure her that this was not the case. Yet I could make no impression upon her. Thus frustated of her intention—and caring so much for the well-being of her son—the woman sank to her knees and burst into violent sobbing. And she converted me!

Mindful of all the stern admonitions of the fathers and brethren—mindful too of all my theological background—I remembered that God is love, and rejected them all. I could not find it in my heart to believe that this woman would not impart some degree of Christian faith to the son whom she loved so dearly. She obviously believed in God. Would God and his church desert her? A critic might have claimed that she desired her son's baptism for the wrong reasons. But how could the church really discover those reasons? And by what right did the church propose to crucify her for them? I told the woman to go home. I would baptise her child. Six months later, without previous promise or notification, she appeared at her first communicants' class.

During the next year, I baptised one hundred and fifty-two children. The elders became disgruntled. They could see the great procession of parents bringing their babies for baptism. They took note of the fact that on the Sundays appointed for the admission of new communicants, there were often more unfamiliar faces in the church than familiar ones. They wondered, however, why they did not see these faces again except at the communion service or at the occasional evening service of worship. They had no idea of the time and effort which these baptismal interviews demanded, and they refused to acknowledge the various factors which made regular attendance difficult if not impossible for many young families. They did see, on the other hand, that the church was far from full on an average Sunday morning and that, consequently, the offering plates were half-filled as well. Some felt disappointed, some were hurt, while some, in anger, expressed the opinion that these baptismal parties were 'making mugs' of the church and its leaders. What none of us had initially perceived was that, in making use of the act of baptism as a means of evangelisation, we had set our course to bring men and women to Jesus Christ.

More and more I was beginning to understand that conversion to Christ need not mean—and sometimes could not mean—attendance at church. In Niddrie, at any rate, evidence of a strong faith did not necessarily mean a corresponding seat at the morning worship service. The consequences of this growing realisation ultimately determined the direction which our 'team' would take in the parish of Richmond Craigmillar.

CHAPTER FIVE

The Shape of my Church

Two hundred and fifty-three members had signed the call to bring me to Richmond Craigmillar. If I had been a reasonably perceptive person, I should have recognised that this was an indication of problems to come. More than eight hundred names appeared on the Communion Roll.

The induction occurred on a Summer's night. Less than half the seats in the church were occupied. This did not particularly perturb me. I reasoned that a good many of the congregation must still be away on holiday. However, the following Sunday told the same story. During the singing of one hymn, I took the time to count heads. Only one hundred and fifty men and women were worshipping. I was to discover that this was a good congregation for Richmond Craigmillar. Obviously, attendance at morning worship was going to present one of our greatest problems in the future.

Attendance at divine worship has a peculiar significance in the Church of Scotland. Morning and evening services not only have to do with the affairs of God, they also have much to do with the affairs of man. Unless people come to worship in the Kirk, people do not give money to the Kirk. If people do not give money to the Kirk, it becomes impossible to pay the minister his stipend, heat the building and care for its maintenance. An examination of the current financial statement revealed that £1,500 had been given to Richmond Craigmillar during the past year. Half of this had been collected in the offering plate. The other half had been assembled through an assortment of jumble sales, garden fetes and whist drives. The total sum was far less than was needed to meet the basic expenses of the church. Richmond Craigmillar, therefore, had become dependant upon the Home Board of the Church of Scotland to pay for what it could not afford. In 1965, it could not afford the services of a full-time minister, much less raise the money to meet the salaries of an assistant and a deaconess. Financially, it was as much a dependant church as any product of the Church Extension Scheme. Yet it had full status.

Something had to be done. Present members needed to be made aware of their responsibilities to the church. New members had to be sought. Yet this was easier said than done. The church was not an important part of the community life in Niddrie. A benevolent institution, it provided certain services for those who sought them. It arranged baptisms, weddings and funerals. It provided regular diets of worship. It was a final court of appeal for those who had been turned away by the National Assistance. But in none of these matters did the life of the church make contact with the lives of its parishioners. Somewhere in the history of the Scots people—or of the Niddrie community in particular—a great gap had appeared. Although many people could truth-fully profess their faith in Jesus Christ, only a handful acknowledged that this faith might lead them into the corporate life of the Christian Church.

I began with the worship services and the structures of the church itself. Obviously, if an impact was to be made upon the community, the life of the church would need to be the life of Jesus Christ. The message of Christ's love would need to be the purpose which motivated everything undertaken at Richmond Craigmillar. Perhaps then the people would see and understand. Perhaps then the parishioners would flock to their church.

Difficulties immediately presented themselves. Although Richmond Craigmillar might be an unknown entity to the thousands who lived within the parish, it was very much the personal preserve of the one hundred and fifty members who came along faithfully to its morning worship service once a week. These faithful few found their resistance to change supported and even strengthened by the structures of religious life and worship which were characteristic of the church as a whole. The morning worship service, for instance, was a long, dreary affair which seemed fashioned for folk who had been taught to endure worship rather than to participate in it. Many of the people could not even understand the meaning of the words which they sung Sunday after Sunday, yet they sturdily resisted any alternatives. Should any attempt be made to alter the structure of 'their' Service, then great mutterings were to be heard from the older members about 'the tradition of the Church of Scotland'. What a claim! In just four centuries, 'the tradition of the Church of Scotland' had included archbishops, superintendants, and 'No Popery'. In any case, the erection of any 'tradition' between Christ and his people was a direct denial of the meaning of 'Protestant'. However, resistance to change in regard to the morning worship service remained intractable. Although given the power to alter it, I felt that to alienate the few remaining members of the congregation in this early stage of my ministry might mean total disaster. I left the morning worship service alone.

The evening worship service was another matter. Only half a dozen people—and sometimes less— trotted along to worship on a Sunday night. If the morning service was difficult to endure, the sound of six voices croaking about a triumphant city of God in the midst of a cavernous empty church appeared altogether ridiculous. If we couldn't do better than this, sound economics dictated the closure of the church on a Sunday evening. Even the elders subscribed to this view when they took a look at the heating bills. They allowed me to proceed with an attempt at innovation.

Obviously our evening worship was going to be a small and intimate affair. It seemed wise, therefore, to emphasise the aspect of communication between the preacher and his congregation. I began to construct a service with two contrasting models in mind: actor and comedian. An actor is a fellow who has learned his lines and recites them. He depends upon his playwright for what he has to say. His audience may be composed of businessmen or bus-conductors, but he still has the same lines to recite. He asks his audience to enter in to the spirit of the play which he is acting. Many a worship service is recited like a play in which the minister has become the actor. Unfortunately, the acting is often fairly mediocre! The clergyman enters the pulpit with his text prepared and proceeds to expound the written document. No matter what may be the nature of his eloquence, no matter how many rehearsals he has undertaken to convey the impression of spontaneity, he is still confined to his text. A comedian, on the other hand, locates the identity of his audience. He pays attention to the people who are sharing the room with him. He 'warms them up' with a couple of jokes. He makes mental notes about the composition of the group in front of him. More and more, as the hour progresses, he becomes a part of that group, adapting his language, though not necessarily his content, to meet their needs. This is the nature of communication. It is exchange.

In Niddrie, it seemed impossible to forecast adequately just what type of a group might come along to worship on a Sunday evening. Since social patterns made frequent attendance difficult on a Sunday night, one group of worshippers might be composed chiefly of young people: teenagers or married couples. Another Sunday night, the group might be composed of old age pensioners or a mixture of old and young. It seemed appropriate therefore to adopt the technique used by a comedian—to explore the nature of each evening congregation by a series of quips and jokes which often, before the service has finished, had become a dialogue between the minister and his congregation. The whole affair demanded therefore some improvisation. Several constituents of worship remained stable: a Scripture reading, prayers and either a talk or a discussion. Although I committed the outline of the service to memory, the words which I used were 'off the cuff' in order to communicate all the better with the particular group of worshippers which had come along. Songs, stories and anecdotes were often used as well. It was a comic's technique with a most serious purpose.

I recall that it was my father who had given me my first lesson in the art of verbal communication. In our little town in Missouri, he was often in demand as a public speaker. He spoke at political rallies and community meetings. He was frequently called upon to be an after-dinner speaker. On all of these occasions, he managed to clothe his purpose in words which communicated that purpose to the group which he was addressing. He did it so naturally that no one ever guessed the work that he expended in preparation. For each talk, he made elaborate notes. Then he constructed a tight organisation. And then he would withdraw to a quiet backroom and, through the closed door, the rest of the family could hear him talking. He was talking through his speech; listening to the sound of his own words. Facts he committed to memory; some statistics were carefully noted. But the rest of his address was not in his papers nor in his mind, but in his ears and in his mouth.

As a teenager, I had been asked to give my first public address at a school gathering. I was petrified. I wrote down every word and laboriously committed it to memory. When it was finally delivered, the applause was lukewarm. I hadn't made a mistake, but I had failed completely to communicate with the audience.

That night, my father offered me some sound

advice. He did so hesitantly, because I was a prickly teenager. He suggested that I 'talk-through' the subsequent speeches that I deliver, that I learn to listen to the sound of my own voice. This was the type of preparation that I began to use now for the evening worship service at Richmond Craigmillar. I left many 'open ends', preferring to try to find the right words which would be adequate for communication on the particular evening on which the talk was to be given. In any case, there had to be room for the Holy Spirit to make himself heard. And often, to my utter amazement, that was precisely what did take place, filling me with an eloquence which was not my own possession. Hitherto, I had polished every theological phrase till it sparkled. One never knew but that the Professor of Divinity might be present at some evening diet of worship! But these written phrases communicated nothing to our local people. Neither did the quotations from the poets or the philosophers. Instead, as my involvement within the parish increased, I was able to make reference to events and activities which told of God's work within the local neighbourhood. I was in the process of becoming a real preacher.

In these evening worship services, we were also able to dispense with some of the more familiar 'stage props'. Since flowing robes and preaching gowns simply got in my way I wore a suit. I dispensed with the use of the pulpit as well. The great blasts of our electronic organ and the hymns of the nineteenth century seemed unhelpful in our task of communication. Instead, we adopted the negro spirituals and folk music which had served as the basis for contemporary 'pop' music. These songs were effectively accompanied on a single guitar by Duncan Nicholson, a member of the congregation. The last thing that I was looking to do was to be 'trendy' or 'with it'. The object of the exercise was not to fill the Kirk with screaming teenagers. I simply hoped to be able to share the message of the Christian gospel with a small group of people. The old people liked it as well as the young! Most folk in fact prefer to share in the process of communication than be 'addressed'. Consequently, our numbers on a Sunday night rose to between fifty and seventy. That was about right. Many more and this type of worship service would have no longer been effective.

The structures of the church also revealed a marked resistance to change. Nominally, the Kirk Session had included seventeen members at the time of my induction. In reality, however, a number of these elders had fallen quietly by the wayside. For pastoral purposes, this number was totally inadequate. Elders of the Church of Scotland are asked to attend Sunday worship, to attend appropriate meetings and to visit a 'district' (a localised group of names which appear on the congregational roll). Several elders were being required to visit some forty houses in Craigmillar. No-one seemed particularly concerned about this. Yet no working man could possibly do pastoral justice to forty people, many of whom were sick or elderly. He just didn't have the time.

Session meetings also proved difficult. Most of the elders at Richmond Craigmillar were working men with little experience of policy-making or the technique of constructive debate. All the same, the structure of the Church of Scotland imposed upon them the responsibility for the whole direction of Richmond Craigmillar parish church. Little wonder that some times they became frustrated! Their frustrations often spilled over into the Session meetings. Frustrations in their personal lives and in their church-life made for angry words and lifted voices. I did not look forward to our Session meetings. Often it seemed that, by virtue of my position as moderator, I was pitted against the entire Kirk Session, like a representative of mid-management fighting off a pack of shop stewards. And they had got me where they wanted me. I was their employee! One man in particular would often turn a brilliant shade of scarlet and wave his fist in my direction. I took good care to station a table between the two of us. However, in the end, the whole affair was not to be taken too seriously. The day after the Session debate, all would be forgotten and the elders would have become the amiable men that they had been prior to the meeting. Yet I was often left shattered emotionally.

Perhaps it was not unusual that, early in the course of my ministry at Richmond Craigmillar, I should have had some reflections about the nature of the eldership. The best thing that could be said about our Session meetings was that they provided a form of emotional release for the participants. Little business got done. They were basically good-hearted to me. But the meetings appeared to bring out the worst in them. My solution therefore was to have fewer meetings and to direct the attention of the Kirk Session towards the pastoral needs of the congregation. Obviously we had to acquire more elders in order to do this adequately. Turning through the pages of the communion roll, I discovered the names of fifty men who might qualify as candidates. By visiting, and even cajoling, I was able to add the names of eight to the Session roll during the course of the first year. Subsequently, still more were added. It would be foolish to claim that these men considered themselves to be leaders of the Kirk. They were not asked to be leaders. They were, however, asked to demonstrate a genuine pastoral concern for the men and women who composed the congregation. They were asked to visit regularly with special attention to the sick and the infirm. Each elder was asked to contact an appropriate member of the team if he felt that one or another required special attention. On the whole, the system worked admirably and it helped to break down any tensions which might have existed between the Kirk Session and the team.

In all of these ways, the shape of our church began to emerge during the first years of my ministry. It was a church with two types of worship service. It had a Kirk Session of working men who showed care and compassion to their fellow members. It was also a church which had begun to attract people. During 1965, almost one hundred new communicants were admitted to membership in the church. This was followed by even greater numbers in the following year. Some of these new faces were older people, but the majority was composed of teenagers or young married couples. Many had been attracted to Richmond Craigmillar by the evening service. As the deaconess remarked,

'It's just an old-fashioned missionary service with folk music instead of Moody and Sankey'.

It was difficult to find the best way to prepare these new communicants for participation in the church. I had found my own way to Jesus Christ with little help from church structures of classes of any kind. In my youth, through occasional exposure to a Protestant Sunday school, I had formed my own opinion of 'Gentle Jesus, Meek and Mild'. He appeared to me to have been a kindly 'do-gooder' who travelled about the country-side with a lamb tucked under his arm. Not the kind of fellow to make small boys sit up and take notice! Later, at university, I found God through prayer and meditation. After reading extensively in Chinese and Indian philosophy, I was compelled to take up the New Testament in order to write an essay for a required course in Religion. I read *The Gospel according to Mark*. Imagine my amazement! Here was a real man, not the Sugar Plum Fairy, who knew anger and frustration, and also sorrow, suffering and pain. Here was a man who was also something more than a man, who spoke with authority of the God whom I already knew through my own prayers. He answered the questions of my heart. The New Testament was also the story of the early Church. I turned to find the Church in the twentieth century and was confronted by a bewildering variety of structures. I began with the Roman Catholic Church and studied with a priest for a number of months. When my instruction convinced me that Roman Catholic structures were often based more firmly on Tradition rather than on Scripture, I turned to the Presbyterian Church in

America. Perhaps it was naivete—perhaps only a desire for honesty—but it seemed appropriate to me that Christ's Church should reflect the teachings of Jesus of Nazareth. Or at least should attempt to do so.

Most of our new communicants approached the church with as little theological knowledge as I had possessed. What they did have was faith. Since the Apostles' Creed and the Westminster Confession appeared to be historically and culturally inappropriate for the Niddrie folk, I made use of a revised version of a catechism drafted by Dietrich Bonhoffer as the basis for our new communicants' classes. These classes were lively and brief. I was aware that no amount of formal instruction could impart a thorough knowledge of the teachings of the Church to people who had come along to become new members. In any case, I didn't have all the answers myself, nor did my church. After many classes, I reflected that I had learned more from the faith which these new communicants brought to our discussions than I had been able to teach them. I saw these classes as opportunities for all of us to *share* our faith. What was important was that these people had found the confidence to come forward and to state that faith. In a community which had little admiration for the church and little knowledge of Jesus Christ this was no easy matter. It was my hope that understanding and comprehension of the missionary purpose of the church would come to these new communicants through participation in its life and worship.

We had begun our work. Men and women were being brought to Christ. They were accepting the responsibilities of membership in his Church. Slowly, the structures of congregational life were being altered. My hope was that, eventually, every member of Richmond Craigmillar might find the courage and the faith to take up the cross daily in a difficult community and follow wherever the Saviour might lead.

CHAPTER SIX

A Place in the Sun

'What do you want here?'

The question was a hostile one. So was the questioner. He was standing next to me by the football pitch. Evidently he had just finished work in the Newcraighall Colliery, for his features were partially obscured by the grime of the coal pit.

I had strolled over to the park to watch a 'friendly' football game between two miners' teams. Engrossed in the play, I had quite forgotten that my clerical collar made me A Marked Man.

'I've just come along to watch the game' I replied, and walked away along the line. The miner viewed my retreating figure with suspicion. Clearly, he regarded me as an outsider. Was I hoping to poach players for some future church football team? Was I trying to make a place for the church within the thriving mining community? Was I out to convert him? Whatever his inward thoughts, this fellow and his companions from the coal pits made it clear throughout the rest of the game that my presence was definitely not needed, and unwelcome.

In 1965, coal-mining was still the greatest single means of employment for the men of Niddrie. For generations this had been the case. As it had been in the days of Hugh Miller, so it was one hundred and fifty years later. Every day witnessed a steady procession of miners making their way to the coal-pits which ringed the parish: Newcraighall, Woolmet and Monktonhall. Although working conditions had improved as the years had passed, I never met a miner who could tell me truthfully that he enjoyed working down the pit.

Coal-mining, however, was not simply a means of employment in Niddrie. It was also the open door to a closed society. 'Miners take care of their own', the miners often said proudly. The phrase served as a motto for a flourishing welfare society. For the young, there were the youth clubs and football teams which were the pride of the parish. For the old, there were a variety of welfare associations and recreational activities. For the miners and their families, there were social clubs which were so popular within the district that their waiting-lists for membership contained hundreds of names. At the heart of the community was the society which the miners had created for themselves.

These men would brook no interference from the church in their affairs. They felt that the church was hypocritical. It had arrived too late with its offers of help. Although a Parliamentary Commission of 1840 had found no evidence of children at work in the Newcraighall pit, for instance, it spoke of old colliers who could recall the days when they had been 'slaves'. What had the Church been doing to help the miners during these difficult times? Nothing. Government legislation had been slow to help as well. So the miners had looked after themselves. They had done a good job so far, and they would continue to do so. They even had their heroes. The name of Abe Moffat was dear to the heart of every man in the pits. Of course they were not averse to making use of the Welfare State, availing themselves of all its benefits. They treated the doctors and social workers with contempt, inventing back-aches or social disabilities which might add a pound or two to the weekly pay-packet. For security itself, however, the miners looked neither to the church nor to the state. It was enough for them to know that 'miners take care of their own'.

I had not been long in Niddrie before I began to realise that to fail to gain a foothold within this closed society would always place me on the periphery of the life of the community. If I was going to be able to deliver the message of the gospel, I would have to gain the attention and perhaps even the respect of the miners. Pulpit oratory seemed unlikely to command much interest. Few miners ever stepped inside a church. Deeds and actions, however, might be a more convincing way of conveying the message of Christ. How was this to be done? How were these men and women to be best told that Christ had died for them, that his Church was a community which had been created for them and that it was not an alternative to the society of miners but a way of enhancing their fellowship together? Occasionally, the newspapers would carry a story about the visit of a parish minister to a pit. This seemed to me to be quite false. I could never become a member of the mining community. For a start, I lacked the abilities necessary to train as a coal-miner. I did not believe for a moment that I could ever move within the ranks of the miners as an equal, enduring all their hardships, facing all their risks. Even suppose that I had managed to do this, becoming a member of the mining community would not necessarily allow me to demonstrate to the miners the saving love of Jesus Christ. What I was seeking instead was an avenue of communication, some way for the gospel to sound its message. The answer to my problem came in a most unexpected manner.

One Saturday afternoon in October, I officiated at the wedding of a young couple who had attended the church from time to time during the two preceding months. During the ceremony, I could not help noticing one young fellow who sat with his wife and children close to the front of the church. Throughout the service, he sat grinning away merrily as if to demonstrate that he considered the whole procedure to be a piece of nonsense. Later, at the wedding reception, he was introduced to me. His name was Douglas Dobson. He was the bride's brother, a coal-miner, and he lived in the heart of Niddrie. Dougie maintained that the church was rubbish. His mother had died recently and the officiating minister had cared so little about the funeral service that he had not taken the time to discover whether it was a man or a woman that he was burying. And the church said that it cared! Dougie dismissed Christianity as a bad joke. It was much better to be a communist, he maintained. We had a bit of an argument. He told me that I was ignorant about the ways of working-men, which was true. I told him that, for a communist, he was also remarkably ignorant since he was almost totally unfamiliar with the teachings of Marx or Lenin. A dimly remembered *Das Kapital* helped me to hold up my end of the discussion. It was conducted in such good humour, however, that we agreed to meet again. I was going for a swim in a couple of days and Dougie agreed to meet me at the Portobello swimming baths.

The Portobello swimming baths are big and deep and full of cold salt-water. I really went along for the hot shower afterwards. I had worked out that the whole process was much cheaper than using my immersion heater at the manse and, in any case, it was much more enjoyable. Dougie met me outside the baths. As soon as we were inside, he challenged me to a race. I jumped into the water and swam across the deep end of the pond. Behind me, I could hear evidence of Dougie's entrance into the water as well. However, when I reached the other side and looked back to find him, I could find no-one behind me. Gradually, however, my near-sighted eyes focused upon some thrashing in the centre of the baths. Convinced that Dougie was joking, I swam over to see what all the commotion was about. When I reached the middle of the pond, Dougie was nowhere to be seen. Then he surfaced. One look was enough to convince me that he was in serious trouble. In his panic, he grabbed at my throat and we both went under, Dougie on top of me. We struggled beneath the surface. My lungs were bursting for air. At last I forced him to release his hold. Both of us came to the surface and, by good fortune, I rose behind him. Seizing his chest with my left arm and guided by some dim recollection of Red Cross training, I slowly pulled him over to the side of the baths. Both of us were gasping for breath.

As I reached the edge, I looked up and caught sight of the baths attendant; he was seated, reading a comic.

From that moment onward, Dougie and I were fast friends. Although I didn't make much of the incident, he never lost an opportunity to tell his mates (mostly coalminers) about what had taken place during our first swim together. Undoubtedly, the story must have grown with the telling. As a result, I began to receive a more friendly reception from the mining community. Many of Dougie's pals would call at his home from time to time. I always hesitated to come in when any of these friends had arrived before me. I did not want to abuse Dougie's hospitality. Yet the communist would insist that I take a seat among his working mates from Newcraighall colliery.

'Come on in,' he would say impatiently; and then, with pride to the assembled company, 'This is Bill.'

If if had looked for deference or respect, I would not have found it in Dougie's home. What I did discover was *acceptance*, of myself and of my vocation. Gradually the miners began to accept me as well. No longer did they think that it was peculiar to sit down and have a discussion with a clergyman. Our discussions were far-ranging, dealing with almost every conceivable subject. The more we talked, the more we learned about one another. The miners learned about the direction which I was hoping our church might take within the district. I learned a great deal about the miners' values and about their attitude to the Christian faith.

In many respects, Dougie was typical of the Niddrie miners. In his attitude to the Christian faith, he was completely representative. He could not separate the Christian faith from the church in his own mind. In our discussions, any mention of Jesus Christ was quickly translated into ecclesiastical terminology. Dougie didn't know anything about Jesus Christ but he did know a bit about the church. He remembered bitterly how the minister who had buried his mother had not even known that he was her son. He remembered humorously how an elder of the church had gone from door to door asking for an offering, the first pastoral visit that Dougie had received. These were the only two ways in which the Church in the name of Jesus Christ had touched Dougie's life. How ineptly it had done so! Since he had no love for this Church, he could not accept Jesus Christ. He would not attend a morning worship service therefore; he could not bring his children to be baptised. Yet he would accept me as a friend.

I was happy myself to have that friendship. Dougie's home became a place of refuge, a harbour where a warm fire and a cup of tea were always waiting. Many nights, long after 11 p.m., I would stop in for a chat on the way back from pastoral visitation. The warmth of the fellowship which I found in Dougie's home helped to make the cold and lonely manse a little more bearable. Dougie himself was frequently characterised as a 'hard man' by those who knew his reputation within the community. Now twenty-seven years of age, he had already endured a terrible accident below the surface of the mine which had half-buried him under tons of earth and rock. He had few illusions about life, was always willing to ask the local doctor to 'give him a line' for an extra week's holiday (with compensation), and lectured me repeatedly for spending too much time with the 'lay-abouts' and 'wasters'. However, he was always ready to work together with other men from the pit to assist in a new youth-club venture or to undertake some task to aid the old-age pensioners. Knowing Dougie and his friends was like knowing the whole of the mining community in miniature. As my knowledge grew, I became aware that beneath the coal dust and the thick skins beat warmer hearts than I had previously encountered in any society.

The fellowship of the coal-miners was a fellowship which often put the Church to shame. There was a generosity of spirit among the miners which had little to do with the gossip and back-biting which were sometimes characteristic of the local congregation. All the same, I had not come to proclaim the gospel of the Church but the gospel of Jesus Christ. That gospel of love and redemption judges all human benevolence and finds it to be wanting, even such kindness as was manifested by the miners in 'taking care of their own'. In the discussions which took place in Dougie's sitting-room, I tried to be as honest with them as they were with me. What a difference Jesus Christ could make to their own lives, to the community, to the Kirk! As our mutual respect increased, I found that I no longer regarded their acceptance of me as a novelty. It appeared that, within our own community, members of the church of Richmond Craigmillar and workers in the New-craighall Colliery were pursuing many of the same ends.

Two years later, Dougie and his family emigrated

to Canada. There they have done very well for themselves. Just before their departure, all of the family gave me a special gift: They appeared, unannounced and unexpected, at a morning worship service. Two days later, they had gone, leaving Niddrie far behind. However, they had left behind another gift as well. Through their friendship, they had opened up pathways of understanding and acceptance to my ministry within the parish. In later years, various members of the church were heard to protest because they believed that I was not held in respect by the local people. No-one called me 'Mr Christman', they complained. Too many parishioners stopped at the church-door to ask for 'Bill'. I had learned, however, that the basis for communication within the community was not this bogus type of respect but instead acceptance and mutual understanding. As one local resident put it to me: 'You've become one of our ane folk'. And that was enough.

CHAPTER SEVEN

Making a Start

In 1965, a visitor's first impression of life in Niddrie invariably had to do with children. Throughout the length and breadth of the parish the supply of young people was always plentiful. There were children everywhere. Early in the morning, groups of toddlers roamed the streets, kicking the broken glass impatiently out of the way as they organised their own pre-school play activities. By eleven o'clock, groups of delinquent boys stood waiting for the pub's door to open while younger children hung back, hoping to be thrown the odd penny. On an afternoon, many teenagers stood listlessly in the closes, idle through lack of employment. As the sun began to set, the pavements would become thronged with children coming home from school, hanging out of the windows, shouting to one another, gathering round the mobile chip-shop for an evening 'meal'; children crawling over automobiles left derelict by their former owners, attacking one another with sticks and staves, wandering and waiting and hoping for the Great Miracle to occur which would allow them to become individuals—to assume personalities and to defy the whole pattern of existence which determined what they should be and what they should become. But the miracle always failed to take place. . . .

Douglas Templeton's task was to make contact with these children. It was not an easy job. He had to wait until the children wanted to make contact with him. He could not make a move to initiate the procedure himself. This was the lesson which I had learned from my experience as a Youth Leader seven years prior to my arrival in Niddrie. In the Summer of 1958, the United Presbyterian Church of America had sent me to work as youth leader in a tiny community situated in the mountains of West Virginia. Although I had supervised a recreation programme for small children within the district, my chief task had been to make contact with the older teenagers in the vicinity. These youngsters would rendezvous every night at the 'Clear Creek'. They would gather there to talk, to tell stories and to throw stones into the swiftly-flowing water below. They were all very poor. Their parents had somehow been isolated from the progress and prosperity generally associated with American life. Within the small community there was widespread unemployment and lack of education. Frequent intermarriage between the families who had lived for so long in the mountains had produced a number of mentally retarded children as well. These youngsters—poor, illiterate, and painfully shy—gathered together each night to make common cause against a world which cared nothing for them. They wanted nothing to do with outsiders. They resented the presence of strangers.

Night after night, I would join the group of teenagers which had gathered beside the waters of the Clear Creek. I found myself marked as an outcast. No-one would speak directly to me. Many of the local boys would talk about me, telling jokes at my expense or laughing at me among themselves. Not one teenager, however, took me aside to ask about my welfare. No-one even bothered to ask me what had brought me to the Clear Creek in the first place. I had never felt so much alone. I was determined, however, not to approach them. Somehow I knew that any bridge of communication would have to originate with the young people themselves. Night followed night. I despaired. I was certain that I would never be able to fulfil the task which had been given to me. Finally, one evening, one of the boys came across to the place where I was seated.

'My family and I have been talking', he said, 'We was wonderin' would you like to come and spend the weekend with us?'

I ran all the way back to my 'digs' to get the clothes that I would need for the weekend! It was the most joyous journey of my life. When I rejoined the boy, I asked him what had prompted the invitation. He shrugged his shoulders:

'We just thought it was a good idea', he said.

His 'good idea' helped me to fulfil my assignment at Clear Creek. Although the roof leaked directly over my bed and thirteen of us were crowded into two and one-half rooms, I enjoyed the weekend thoroughly. Once this break-through had been accomplished, I found myself accepted by the other teenagers as well. The rest of the Summer was a story of camp-fires and swimming expeditions, of fishing holes and hunting trips. I explored abandoned mineshafts with the boys and found myself listening to their guitar music on the mountain tops. I had made my contact. The waiting-game had at last paid off. During the weeks that followed, I was able to increase the number of my acquaintances until they included almost every young person who lived in the vicinity of the Clear Creek.

There were many similarities between the situation which I had experienced in West Virginia and that which confronted us in Niddrie in 1965. Many of the young people who lived in the parish felt that they had a common grievance against society. They had no love for outsiders. Defiantly, they expressed this feeling in the slogan which defaced many of the walls: 'Niddrie Rules the World'. Discussing the problem with Douglas, we concluded that the best policy was patience. He could play the waiting-game as well. Living in the district, he was always available to the local youngsters if they wished to seek him out. They could find him standing at the corner, waiting at the local shop or queueing for a bus. They could see him running for shelter in a downpour or stretching his large frame out in the grass in order to get the benefit of an hour's sunshine. Quite naturally, however, they were suspicious. What sort of person was this fellow, who spoke with a public school accent yet lived in the centre of Niddrie Mains Terrace? What did he want with them? While they wondered, Douglas waited. As I had once despaired, so did he now. For the first three months, it appeared that our experiment would fail completely and that he would never be able to achieve the contact with young people that he was seeking.

Suddenly, one week, Douglas reported that progress was being made. Groups of youngsters were calling at his house, seeking him out. At first they only came to 'try him on', to see if and where he would draw the line in his relationships with them. It was a type of bear-baiting. Often it took the form of banter and Douglas found himself to be the butt of their jokes. The youngsters played tricks on him, took advantage of his good nature and ridiculed him to their friends. Nothing could break the man's integrity. Eventually their respect for him began to grow. Should a teenager be in need, Douglas was his friend. If he was asked to chum a lad to court, undoubtedly he would eventually conduct the boy's defence personally. If a group of fellows asked him for a lift in his old motor to the swimming baths, he might well arrange to go along with them on the outing. If a girl was 'in trouble', he would see that she and her baby received proper care. If a boy was unemployed, Douglas would move heaven and earth—even the chocolate factory or the brick works if need be—to find him a job. As he gradually gained the confidence and trust of the young people who lived within the district, so he also began to gain the respect of their parents as well. Over cups of tea in many local homes and over pints of beer in many local public houses, Douglas became the friend of all who lived within the vicinity. Once, I asked him if he did not feel that he was being 'used' by the people of Niddrie. He answered after time for reflection, taking a draw on his ever-present pipe:

'But that is why we are here.'

Douglas was in Niddrie in order to be 'used'. He was not a trained social worker or youth leader. He had not studied to be a lawyer. He did not want to usurp the positions of professional people who had these qualifications. To Douglas, however, had been given a different task: the task of care and compassion. Whether a man was a criminal, or a woman a prostitute, made no difference to him. His ministry was to all men and women regardless of their circumstances. Before the Corporation housing officials and within the Sheriff's Court, he made this quite clear. In the words of a local Catholic priest, he had become the 'father confessor' to all of the people in his immediate neighbourhood, regardless of their religious affiliation.

Some of the younger children approached Douglas from time to time with a view to attending the church worship service or with a request regarding the Sunday school. Douglas always brought them along. Shortly before Christmas, one group of children came to him and asked if they could put on a Christmas play. Douglas was delighted. It was decided that the children's play should be produced at the evening service on the Sunday prior to Christmas. Rehearsals began at once.

This was to be a play about the birth of the Christ-child. It was written, acted and directed by the children themselves, aged seven to eleven. On the Saturday prior to the performance, the dress rehearsal took place. Everything went well until the advent of the Wise Men. The first Wise Man, a little girl with a great beard of cotton, marched all the way down the centre aisle of the church. She placed her gift before the Christ-child and stepped back:

'I bring you gold', she said.

The second Wise Man, a little boy dressed in an enormous bathrobe, walked down to the front of the church. He, too, placed his gift before the manger, stepped back and with a loud voice declared:

'I bring you. . . Frankenstein!'

These younger children enjoyed coming along to the church, especially to the evening service with its folk songs and guitar music. Eventually they became the nucleus of an expanding youth fellowship. The older teenagers, however, had little to do with the church. The emphasis on authority and discipline which they found in the Boys' Brigade and Boy Scouts alienated them. There were several other youth clubs in the area but, in order to preserve their very existence, they had been forced to emphasise order and discipline. The local Community Centre articulated a policy of 'No Young People', and this evidently included anyone under the age of thirty. Only the Adventure Playground appeared to offer an alternative. During these years, however, it catered only for children of Primary School age. As a result, many young people walked the streets of Niddrie.

Douglas sought various means of recreation which would be of interest to these 'unattached' teenagers. Surveying the interests which they possessed, he hit upon football as the activity most likely to attract a large number of boys with a corresponding contingent of their female supporters. Football was diligently played in Niddrie already. Each of the local schools possessed a football team. Teams for older players fought with one another to capture the best of these footballers, once their studies had been completed. Football in Niddrie, for this reason, had become a highly selective sport. Only excellent players were likely to find a place in the highly skilled teams sponsored by local groups such as the Miners' Welfare or the Hearts' Supporters Club. Other teenagers, although interested in the game, were not so fortunate. They were left to roam the streets.

Douglas began with a group of these lads. Selecting some of the boys who had come together to play football on a waste piece of ground within the housing estate, he proceeded to make them into a football team. The local Hearts' supporters donated a set of strip and the Edinburgh Corporation allowed them to train one night per week in one of the primary schools. At first, the boys only played 'friendly' games with other clubs in the city. These 'friendly' games, however, aroused so much local support that it was not long before another group of lads had come forward with a request that Douglas make them a team as well. At last, Douglas entered his first team, Richmond Star, in a Football League competition. Mindful of the ages of his boys, he decided upon participation in the league which was organised for lads in their late teens: the Edinburgh Juveniles. Unfortunately, Douglas had no idea that this was one of the toughest leagues in the city. When the Niddrie boys came up against the picked players of the other football teams, the result was disastrous.

Newspaper headlines chuckled, ' "I'm really a left back", said the goalkeeper who has been beaten 109 times in only six games'—this was the caption in an edition of the *Scottish Daily Mail*. The *Edinburgh Weekly* called them the 'City's Soccer Oliver Twists'. Douglas knew what he was doing, however, and the team persevered. Occasionally the boys even won a game. As Douglas continued to train his 'underdogs', the boys' football ability increased. So did their respect for him.

In many ways, football offered a constructive way of working with these unattached youngsters. Since the game was played outside on a football pitch, there was little equipment that the boys could break or destroy. It was also a game which taught some constructive social lessons. It taught team-work, for instance. Without team-work, the boys soon learned that it was almost impossible to score a goal. It taught the boys to be on time when a game was to be played. Once the team had been picked and the game had started, the lad who arrived five minutes late had no opportunity to play football, no matter how brilliant a player he might have been. It also taught a modified version of one of the teachings of Jesus: Thou shalt not strike a player in retaliation (if the referee is watching)! Many of these matters might have appeared trivial, but they were in fact extremely helpful to boys who lacked little training in how to cope with society.

Even more important was the group-identity which began to emerge with each football team. Most of the boys were from homes in which there was some degree of social disorder. Several lads had never known their fathers; others had parents who were alcoholics. In some homes there was unemployment; in others anxiety over poor health. The family-group had failed to be a basic source of stability for most of these boys. At a time of adolescent stress, they needed a group which could give them some degree of support. They also needed a group which could teach them some basic social values. The football team fulfilled this need. Douglas, working together with his football players, taught the boys *not to conform to society, but how to deal with society*. Since most of these lads would live out their adult lives in closes containing six families, it was certainly helpful for them to learn how to deal with other people in a social context.

So the football teams prospered. As each group coalesced, the boys began to raise the money to purchase their own football strip. They organised social occasions for their own benefit. Their success attracted the interest of older men who were willing to serve as trainers and managers. These football teams were one answer to the problems of the young people of Niddrie. Douglas had made a good start.

CHAPTER EIGHT

'Black February'

I shall always remember my first February as the parish minister of Richmond Craigmillar. I called it 'Black February'.

The parish was in an ugly mood. Early in the month, Douglas Templeton decided to stroll over to a youth club dance. He did not go along in any official capacity but only to observe the proceedings. Shortly after he arrived, however, a fight broke out on the dance floor. Equipment was damaged in the scuffle and the club leader's nose was broken. The police were called to the scene and the offenders were charged with Assault and Breach of the Peace. As a result, the club was closed. Embittered, the youth leader resigned. The local young people, however, looked forward to the approaching trial with excitement. Threats were made to intimidate the various teenage witnesses. It was rumoured, however, that the chief witness for the prosecution was to be a local minister. This caused confusion. No-one could remember seeing a minister at the dance. Opinion was divided as to whether it was Douglas or the American who was involved. Walking about the darkened streets of Niddrie suddenly became hazardous.

Violence was not the only crime which showed its

face in 'Black February'. The month was also notable for an extraordinary number of robberies within the parish. Burglary was not uncommon in Niddrie. This time, however, the break-in assumed a form which was particularly cruel. If a house proved to contain nothing valuable, then the thieves would leave their calling card—a lighted match. The occupants would return home to find their house in flames. If the burglars failed to gain entry, the result was the same. Petrol was poured through the letter-box and set alight. The long February nights and the prevailing fog gave the criminals good cover. As a result, families would return from parties to discover that their home was in ruins and that they had to search for a place to spend the night. Old Age Pensioners could be found in tears as they watched the memories of a life-time go up in smoke. Tension and anxiety gripped the parish. Ena Finlayson shared the general apprehension. She lived by herself in a house on Niddrie Mains Road. Because her job took her away from her home during many nights of the week, she was particularly vulnerable to this type of vandalism. Douglas and I urged her to move or to take a companion to stay with her during these difficult weeks. She refused. Outwardly she remained quiet and confident. However, she was obviously worried. One night, she telephoned me; the house next to hers was burning.

Confronted with local anger at the situation, the Labour Party called a public meeting to deal with the problem of fire-raising. The Labour councillors convened their meeting on a cold Tuesday night. The issue had brought several hundred people to the Community Centre. Many of these were middle-aged or elderly women. Occasionally, however, one caught sight of a younger face—an unshaven young man or a haggard housewife, her young brood crowding round her knees. Scattered throughout the crowd were 'the Professionals': several headmasters, one or two social workers and the occasional eager young student whose social concern had prompted his journey to Niddrie.

The Chairman began with a statement that the meeting had no political overtones. He continued with a statement of the common problem: local houses were being looted and burned. He concluded with a request that the people address themselves to the issue at hand. Hardly had he finished speaking when the women began. The first wave of comments constituted a response to the crimes which had taken place:

'It's a terrible thing'.

'It isn't safe to go out at night'.

'This place has changed since I came here'.

These statements appeared to remind each member of the meeting about his own particular problems. An elderly man rose to complain that the light bulbs were always being snatched from his stair; it was five minutes before he took his seat. Other people followed his example. A widow said that she lacked a fence in her back garden. As a result, children were always running through her close. A mother of seven described the dampness which affected her home. At this point, many in the crowd who did not possess any specific grievances joined in conversation with their neighbours:

'You only get the rubbish jobs if you come to Niddrie', shouted one woman to her friend sitting several rows in front of her.

'You're right', her friend responded, 'my Joe lost his job when the boss found out that he lived here.'

Meanwhile, the young man was expounding his point of view to any one who would listen. He maintained that the problems of the district were due to the high percentage of Catholics living in the area. From his speech, I gathered that he was a convert to the Free Church. The young housewife, surrounded by her children, maintained a stunned silence in the midst of the mounting uproar.

Time and time again the Chairman made efforts to recall the meeting to its original purpose, only to be silenced by a number of demands for immediate, specific aid. At last, however, he gained enough silence to call upon the headmaster of the local secondary school. The teacher gave his speech:

'There's nothing wrong with Niddrie', he concluded.

This popular statement won general approval. Finally, in desperation, the Chairman handed round sheets of paper. He asked for nominations to form a committee which would investigate the problem of fire-raising in the district. Immediately, the people began to rise from their seats and take their leave. Men and women jostled one another in their hurry. The sheets of paper were left for the custodian to sweep away in the morning. Only a few contained signatures. Most of these were from 'the professionals'.

The consensus on the street corners and the shop fronts the next morning was that it had been a good meeting. Nothing had been done. No problem had been solved; no action had been taken. The people who attended, however, had been given the opportunity to express themselves, to give vent to their emotions—their frustrations, their anger, their ambitions. Perhaps that was all they wanted anyhow.

The crimes continued, however. Richmond Craigmillar did not escape the attention of the thieves. One morning the Church Officer telephoned to ask me to come to the church immediately. A window had been forced open and a small amount of money stolen from the flower box. We were lucky. In Niddrie Mains Terrace, the small United Free Church became a victim of the vandals. Money was stolen, windows were smashed and the communion wine was poured over the Bibles and the church pews. Then matches were lit and soon flames were spreading throughout the little building. Brokenhearted, the struggling congregation surveyed the damage on the following Sunday morning.

Earlier in the year, the manse had been taken over by a group of delinquent boys. Speaking to some lads who had recently been released from Approved School, I mentioned that they would always be welcome at my home. Since the manse was located just outside the parish, it never occurred to me that they would take me up on my offer. The public house was much closer to them. They arrived quite early the next morning, however, bringing a selection of records. The morning after they were there as well. Usually, there were three of these fellows on any given day, but sometimes the number doubled.

After several weeks had gone by, it occurred to me that these boys had adopted the manse as their club. They were bored and idle. It was a comfortable place to spend a morning drinking tea and listening to records. And it cost them nothing. I was determined to break the habit. I didn't have the time to be a regular host and club-master. In any case, I was certain that the best thing that could happen to these lads was to find employment. Most of my attempts to find them jobs, however, came to nothing. The teenagers were unskilled and had criminal records. They didn't really want to work but they enjoyed travelling with me in the car while I visited factory after factory in hopes of securing a job for them. Finally, I was successful. I managed to get a job for one. He was to begin on Monday morning. On Monday afternoon, as I was driving through the parish, I saw the boy leaning against the doorway of a close.

'What's the matter?', I asked, 'Why aren't you working?'

'My Old Man told me I would be better off on the dole', he replied. He was right.

One February morning, the boys arrived at the door again. They had their records with them. Shortly before, a woman had come to the manse to ask me to officiate at the funeral of her husband. She was seated now weeping in the front room, the room which had been used by the lads for their 'Club'. I explained that it was not convenient for the boys to come in at the moment. Since the bereaved woman was within ear-shot of the front door, I did not go into detail. The teenagers, however, were furious. They were being denied the premises which they had come to expect. White-hot with anger, they disappeared into the thick February fog.

Shortly after this, the telephone calls began.

Twice, a voice assured me that my throat would be slit. Once it guaranteed the same fate for my house-keeper. I guessed that the reason for the calls might lie with my refusal of hospitality to the boys. They had never come back to the manse again. Alter-natively, I reasoned with myself, it was possible that the lads responsible for the violence at the youth club were attempting to intimidate a prospective witness for the Prosecution. I shrugged my shoulders and laughed the matter off. When I happened to mention the matter to Dougie Dobson, however, I began to regard the telephone calls more seriously.

'Be careful', he said, 'these people are animals.'

As a result of our conversation, I began to be worried. Worries and depression came easily to me during those weeks. My car was in a local garage for repairs. It had been there for over a month. Day after day, night after night, I walked through the length and breadth of the parish. The weather was terrible —wet, windy and cold. I had a case of 'flu, then a bad cold, then another bout of 'flu. It seemed to me that 'Black February' would never end.

One night I called by Dougie's house after an evening spent in pastoral visitation. After a cup of tea, Dougie offered to drive me home. Although a communist, he was the only man in the block to possess a television, a refrigerator and a car. When the Revolution at last took place, he would un-doubtedly be the loser. I thanked him for the lift and waved 'goodbye'. I tried the key in my front door but it would not open. It was after midnight. The neigh-bours were all in bed; there was no one to give me any help. I tried the windows. They were all firmly locked. Perplexed, I walked to the back of the house. The garden door was standing open. As I looked, I could see that the French windows were also ajar. I ran forward and looked inside. As I did so, I groaned out loud. Inside everything was chaos: The study was the first room that I saw. Every piece of furniture in it had been smashed. The desk lay toppled on one side. The typewriter had been thrown into the fireplace. Books had been torn apart and their pages scattered all over the room. The passageway was strewn with pieces of food and spilled drinks. I stumbled over further pieces of broken furniture. I could see from the evidence of candle-wax that fires had been attempted but had failed to light. Three rooms had been destroyed by the vandals in this manner. Evidently they had been disturbed by the sound of the door-bell or a movement from one of the neighbouring houses. Only a single shilling and my transistor radio had been taken. Everything possible, however, had been destroyed.

Heartsick and dazed, I began to clean up the mess. I felt degraded and somehow ashamed. I worked until four in the morning before I went to bed. I had no insurance to meet the cost of the damage and it was obvious that I simply would not be able to replace many of the articles which had been destroyed. Early the next morning, I received a telephone call. This time I recognised the voice. It was one of the boys who had made the manse his 'Club' for so many weeks. He told me the names of the lads who had done the damage. Several were teenagers who had also come along to the club. Others had been involved in the fight at the youth club. Later that day, I confronted the lads with the information without revealing my source. Of course, they denied everything.

Where could I go for help in this situation? The most obvious answer was the police. Without witnesses, however, the police were helpless. Although I now possessed the names of the boys who had very likely been responsible for the vandalism to my home, I could not possibly reveal the name of my informant. The members of the church were no source of support either. Many were shocked that the manse should have been vandalised. Undoubtedly, they concluded that it was all my fault. I had been playing with fire, and come away badly burned. I had handled these 'animals' stupidly. The damage to my possessions had been the result. Perhaps they were right.

The whole affair made me question my ministry seriously. What kind of a minister did I want to be? What kind of a minister was needed in Niddrie? It would not have been difficult to become the type of minister that many people expected me to be: baptising, marrying, burying, visiting, but not interfering with the routine lives which people lived within the parish. There was another way of ministry, however, which seemed to me to be more nearly like that of Jesus of Nazareth. This other way constituted a sustained attempt to understand the people of the parish, living alongside them, and suffering when they suffered, being afraid when they too knew fear. It was also a way of doing what the people did not do, a way of faith and self-sacrificing love. I was certain that this was the way that was needed by the people of the parish. It would be the way of cross-bearing for others in the name of Jesus Christ.

How high a price was I willing to pay for such a ministry? Was I willing to risk burglary, as they risked it night after night? Was I willing to leave the lights burning and the television blaring while I was out on pastoral visits as they did night after night? Was I willing to risk being involved in violence on the streets of Niddrie as they did night after night? They all had to take these risks because they lived where they lived. I had another option. I could go elsewhere. If I wanted truly to be a minister to these people, however, I had to learn to share the lives which they lived. Throughout the remainder of 'Black February', I prayed and prayed. Out of my prayer rose the determination that I would fight for the ministry to which I had been called with every attribute that I possessed. I determined that it would be a real ministry, not a token one. Sharing in the suffering of my people, I would lighten its burden with love. Knowing their various fears, I would cling to my knowledge of the Resurrected Christ, mindful of the fact that when fear of death has been conquered, all fears have been vanquished. I reached these conclusions at the end of 'Black February'. From that moment forward, I did not falter. And neither I nor my team were ever troubled again.

CHAPTER NINE

Getting Away from it All

'I was speaking to a group of children yesterday', remarked Douglas Templeton, 'They said that they had never had a holiday.' We began to consider the possibility of taking small groups of children out of the housing estate for short periods of time.

Ordinarily, the advent of Summer marked an intermission in the lives of most of our parishioners. From June to August, things were quiet in the church. Its organisations were temporarily disbanded, its halls stood empty and its team took personal holidays. The existing youth clubs in the area closed their doors as well. The football season had finished. As a result, when the school holidays arrived, there were fewer activities than usual to occupy the local children; during the period when the greatest number of youngsters had the maximum of leisure time, there was no group or organisation which could cater for their interests.

Shortly before the commencement of the Summer, our team met to discuss the problem. Our decision was to formulate a Summer youth programme. One aspect of this programme would be the creation of holidays for children. A variety of motives lay behind our decision. First, it would be a good opportunity to take children from the streets of Niddrie and give them the experience of another environment. Secondly, helping them to 'get away from it all' might provide a well-deserved break for their parents as well, and thirdly, we were certain that holidays in the country-side could be educational. During our first harvest thanksgiving in the church, it had become apparent that many children thought that the Almighty had created milk in bottles. Some had never seen a cow! They were as certain that beans grew pre-packaged in tins. Niddrie had certainly changed from the days when a stone-mason might spend his leisure hours enjoying the beauties of the country-side.

There was an even more compelling reason behind our desire to create a series of holidays for young people, however. Douglas Templeton had begun to explore the need for stable social groups through his work with football teams. Obviously there were many other young people in the district who had no football skills but who would benefit from such group support as well. A country holiday might provide an opportunity to form such a group. It could only be beneficial, however, if a member of the team would be able to give the time and effort necessary to sustain the group once the holiday had been completed.

We decided, therefore, to try to locate a country cottage which could serve as a site for our holiday programme. It proved difficult to find such a place. We scoured the countryside but had little luck. We found a few cottages for sale, but these were well beyond our financial capabilities. At last I had an idea. At one time, in the good old days when I had been an Assistant Lecturer, I had managed to save enough money to rent a country cottage for the Summer months at Galabank, outside the village of Stow in Midlothian. I wrote to my former landlady and discovered that the house was still unoccupied. She agreed to rent it to us for the use of young people, provided that the church help to redecorate it without cost to her. The Kirk Session agreed to sponsor the project. Many willing hands from the Boys' Brigade and the youth clubs were found to do the work and, in a matter of weeks, the interior of the cottage was repainted. Woodwork and plumbing repairs had been carried out as well. Certainly, the cottage was not ideal for our purposes. Although the view from the house was beautiful, the cottage was one of a row of similar buildings which stretched out along the side of a busy highway. The house contained only two rooms, one up-stairs and another on the ground floor, and a kitchen. There was a common toilet in the back garden for the use of all of the residents in the row of attached cottages. However, our intention was only to bring small groups from Niddrie on holidays to the country-side. For that purpose, our cottage near Stow seemed ideal.

The money for the rent had still to be found, however. Richmond Craigmillar, faced with financial problems of its own, could hardly afford to allocate the necessary £65 for the use of the cottage. I was perplexed but determined that the project should continue. Hastily I wrote a letter to the youth fellowship of the First Presbyterian Church of Joplin, Missouri, my home church. I explained the problem. Six weeks later the money arrived. It had been raised by various work-projects which the American youngsters had undertaken on our behalf.

Now we had a cottage, but we had nothing in it. We needed beds and blankets, dishes and cutlery, chairs and tables and—most of all—a cooker. I appealed to the Home Board of the Church of Scotland for help. It responded with a cheque for £200. Some of this money was used to purchase furniture. The rest was used to help to defray the expenses associated with the project: petrol, coal and electricity. It was anticipated that the children would be asked to provide either their own food or the money with which it could be purchased. We thought it only right that they should make a contribution to the project as well. Requests for help also went out to the various Woman's Guilds within the City of Edinburgh. The response was heartening. For weeks, my telephone rang with offers of aid. They donated most of the blankets, cutlery and dishes necessary to outfit the cottage.

Now we were ready to begin. Our idea was to take small groups of youngsters to the cottage. An ideal ratio was felt to be six children for every adult leader present at the site. We would take the younger children from Monday to Friday in the course of each week since they were temporarily free from school during their holidays. Weekends we hoped to reserve for teenagers whose jobs might prevent them from coming at other times. Ena and Douglas soon had their diaries full of bookings for the use of the cottage. Both were already involved with groups of young people. They viewed these holidays as opportunities to deepen already existing relationships. Since they were willing to pledge so much of their time to the project, it seemed to me that I should be willing to take my turn at the place as well. However, I was not involved with any particular group of young people which could benefit from a holiday away from the Parish.

By the end of June the cottage was ready for use, and had already been booked for most of the Summer. However, it was still free during the first fortnight in July. This was the traditional Edinburgh Trades' Fortnight. During this time, most of the industries and businesses in Edinburgh came to a halt. Many working boys and girls were on holiday. In Niddrie, however, most of these young people lacked the money or the initiative to plan a holiday away from the housing estate. For these reasons, they could invariably be found standing on the street corners, patronising the local betting establishment or chatting idly beside the chip shop. I could have found no better opportunity to begin our holiday experiment.

Mrs Forbes usually offered dinner to Douglas and me after the morning worship service; I always accepted! Walking along Niddrie Mains Terrace after one such occasion, I happened to see a group of lads sitting in one of the closes. They were playing cards. Although I did not know them, I tried to start up a conversation. They smirked. Obviously they did not want their friends to see them talking to a fellow in a clerical collar. I tried my bait:

'It's Trades' Fortnight next week. If you fellows don't have anywhere to go, give me a ring. We've got a cottage you can have for a week or two. The only cost will be the price of your food and drink. I'll drive you down, provide the transport while you're there...and I promise to stay out of your way'.

The boys, all lads in their late teens, looked at me and laughed. They considered that the sting came in the tail of the proposal. When would the minister do his 'Bible-punching', over meals or after lights-out?

'Yeah sure, man,' said one, mimicking my American accent. I gave them my telephone number and beat a hasty retreat. Two days later, the telephone rang. It was Davy, one of the boys.

'We'll go', he said, 'Besides myself, there'll be Dul and Harry, Jock, Twin and Mack'.

On the following Monday morning, the beginning of the Trades, the six lads threw their gear into the boot of my Hillman and piled-in beside me. It was some squeeze, but we made it. Tiny toddlers and old aunties waved 'goodbye' as we set off on our journey.

When we arrived at the cottage, I suggested that we might first allocate the various duties which had to be undertaken. Mack and Harry volunteered to be the cooks. The rest would take turns washing the dishes and sweeping out the house every day. I was to clean out the toilet every morning, a task for which my previous army experience had prepared me. However, when we all discovered that Mack and Harry's best and only dish was tomato soup, we re-allocated the duties. Davy and Dul became the cooks. It was also their task to purchase supplies from our joint fund and to bring them to the cottage. The rest swept and washed. For lads who were normally little involved in the business of housework, it was a remarkable achievement.

On the night we arrived, I experienced the first test of my capacity for leadership; I failed miserably. Since I had little experience with this type of holiday,

I decided initially to make as few rules as possible. In fact, I announced only one: No women in the cottage. The boys were surprisingly agreeable. What I did not know was that they had already located several tents full of females camping in the meadow across the highway from the cottage. Fair enough not to have women in the cottage, they reasoned, but there was no rule to prevent them from crossing the road in order to enjoy the beauties of nature.

As the sun was setting, I heard the sound of a car drawing up outside the building. Into the sitting-room strode five of the biggest and meanest-looking fellows it had ever been my misfortune to encounter. They made The Flintstones look civilised. These were the Big Brothers of my lads.

'You don't mind if we stay the night?' they asked.

Who could refuse? Since there were now not enough beds, I volunteered to sleep downstairs in the sittingroom while the rest bunked above me. Stretching myself delicately over a couple of chairs, I tried to get some sleep. Upstairs I could hear mumbled voices and occasional laughter. As I tossed and turned during the night, I seemed to hear screaming and loud noises from the bed-room. Partly out of fear and partly from sheer exhaustion, I stayed where I was. Finally, I fell into a deep sleep and did not wake until morning.

While I slept inside the house, pandemonium reigned supreme outside. The boys had jumped from their windows to the ground below and crossed to the meadow. There they found the girls. Unfortunately, they also discovered that the young ladies had already been claimed by a group of local lads from Stow. Great fights ensued, a tent was set on fire and feminine screams filled the night. Eventually, having conquered their opponents, the Niddrie lads left the scene, more certain than ever that Niddrie 'ruled the world'. Climbing up the pipes, they fell into their beds and into a deep sleep.

The other residents in the row of cottages had not been so fortunate. Initially the noise from the meadow had awakened them. Now their lights were burning through fear. They had rented these houses in order to escape from the horrors of city life to the peace and tranquillity of the country-side. Incredibly, the city had pursued them all the way to Stow. Thoroughly alarmed, they telephoned for the police. A constable came. At 8 a.m., his knock awakened me. Wearily, I answered his questions. No, I did not know what had happened during the night. Yes, the boys had all gone to bed about midnight. I suggested, after hearing the story of the neighbours' alarm, that he cross the road and question the ladies.

As soon as he left, the boys tumbled down the stairs. They had been listening to the inquisition and were pleased by my answers. Their older brothers had already driven away, promising a return visit. Although the lads claimed total ignorance about the activities of the evening, I remained suspicious. However, when our cooks reminded us that we needed fresh rolls and milk, I volunteered to drive them into the village. There was a sudden rush for the car. All of the boys, evidently, were anxious to leave the vicinity of the cottage. As I reversed, struggling to see over so many heads, one lad shouted, 'Watch out'. At that moment I ploughed into the side of a van which, the night before, had not been positioned directly behind my car: It was the policeman's van. As he charged back across the meadow, I gathered that it was his own personal property. He said that it was practically new, and stared with sadness at the damage I had inflicted. Eventually, after numerous questions on his part and numerous promises on mine, he drove off to the village. The accident had driven the incidents of the previous evening completely from his mind. I, however, would have to pay a high price for his forgetfulness—and my bad driving!

Events at the cottage now settled down into a routine. The boys would sleep through most of the mornings. In the afternoons, they would fish or play cards. Some days we drove to the swimming baths at Galashiels. Once we even made an effort to go pony-trekking. Evenings were spent in the local pubs or dancing in nearby halls. I kept myself apart from these activities as much as possible. For one thing, they were obviously tough characters. For another, my presence certainly would have been inhibiting to them. After all, difficult though it might be for me, this was supposed to be a holiday for them. I wanted them to have a good time.

One evening, the lads all walked off down the road for a pint at the local. As usual, I stayed behind reading. After fifteen or twenty minutes, Davy and Dul returned.

'We've all been talking', said Dul, 'We'd like it if you'd come along with us'.

I was uncertain. Until this time, I had never had a drink in a public house with any member of my parish. I had an idea that many members of the church might disapprove if they discovered that their minister enjoyed a pint. The two lads persisted:

'Don't you *want* to come with us?' asked Davy.

Put that way, I could not refuse the invitation. I walked along with the boys to the bar. Once inside, I found that the boys were pairing off for darts. Although they wanted to include me, I was happy to sit and sip 'Coke'. Since I was near-sighted and the interior of the pub was so dark, I would never have managed to hit the dart-board anyway. Eventually, however, I became bored with my own company. Looking around, I discovered an old piano in a corner of the room. Without thinking much about it, I sat down and played one or two pieces, mostly silent-film music which a veteran of the 'twenties had taught me years before. The sound of applause made me look up from the keyboard. On top of the piano were three pints of lager, two from the boys and one from a local.

'Drink up', shouted the lads, while several of the locals cried for more. Picking up a glass, I drained it, and eventually the others as well. Whether my piano-playing improved much during the course of the evening is debatable. I was a considerably happier man, however, by the time that the pub closed its doors!

Walking back through the village that evening, we all joined in a bit of a sing-song. When we reached the cottage at last, the lads stumbled up the stairs to bed. As usual, I tried to find the most comfortable way to drape my form over two wooden chairs. Five minutes after I had closed my eyes, one of the boys tip-toed down for a glass of water. When he saw the way that I was sleeping—I had not told the lads that I did not have a bed—he woke me up.

'Come on up', he said, 'We can arrange ourselves so that you can have a bunk of your own'.

Gratefully, I obeyed. For the rest of our stay in the cottage at Stow, I was able to sleep in relative comfort. Many nights we would share lengthy conversations before dozing off. The favourite topic was sex. Sometimes, however, the boys would ask me why I had become a minister. I tried to answer them truthfully. The most interesting discussion that we had, however, revolved around the subject of death. For the first time, I began to realise how greatly each one of these tough lads feared the certainty of death. The boys were interested to know how a Christian viewed death. Although some scoffed, others listened. There was free give-and-take. The boys appeared to respect my point of view, even if no one was prepared to admit that he shared it.

Eventually, it became apparent that all of us had become part of a single group. We toured around the country-side, swimming, singing, dancing, horse-back riding. The boys were keen to try anything and everything. We shared all our experiences together. We attempted to work out solutions to our mutual problems. Inevitably, the day for departure drew near. Davy was sad.

'I wish this would never end', he said.

He was not the only one to be sorry that we had to go. Many of the local residents had adopted us. The baker, for instance, always greeted us with gifts of home-baking, even if slightly stale. When I walked into the village each morning, I would invariably return with a great sack of cakes and biscuits on my back. He said that he would miss us. So did the owner of the local cafe. The police constable, however, was not available for comment.

So we returned home, a much different car-load of people than had originally motored to Stow. There were no barriers between us now, no suspicions, no fears. Having cooked and washed, swum and fished in one another's company for ten days, our original relationship had altered entirely. Would this newly-formed structure be strong enough to continue? Now that my usefulness to the boys had finished, would we meet again as strangers? After we returned I saw nothing of them for a fortnight. But one evening Davy and Dul turned up at the Manse.

'The boys want to see you', Davy said.

We made plans to go swimming with the entire group. I was so glad to see them that I even proposed that they should include their older brothers for the occasion! Afterwards, we made arrangements to get together once a week.

I learned a great deal about life in Niddrie from these boys. They introduced me into their homes without embarrassment. Although some were nominal Catholics and others nominal Protestants, not one lad had any contact with a Christian church, let alone the Christian faith. From time to time, I was able to help them a bit. Sometimes, I might drop a hint of advice to one or find employment for another. We stayed together as a group for a number of years. There were other holidays: a weekend in Manchester, a fortnight in Spain. Eventually, as the boys matured, I was able to officiate at their marriage services. Three became members of the church. I was happiest, however, about a remark which Davy made, a remark which was passed on to me after I had left the parish of Richmond Craig-millar:

'If it hadn't been for Bill during those years', he said, 'I'd have been prison-fodder.'

He knew. He understood.

CHAPTER TEN

Missionaries

In Niddrie, we were obviously in a missionary situation. There were many families in spiritual and material need. It was clearly the duty of those who professed to be Christians to take the love of Jesus Christ to such people and to bring them into the Church. This process, however, was not taking place. Instead, some elders spoke contemptuously of the 'animals' who lived in the parish. Although many could quote the teachings of Jesus, they seemed unwilling or unable to apply them to the families who lived in their own stair.

I found this attitude to be very frustrating. Roger Wilson, however, in his book *Difficult Housing Estates* (Tavistock Publications, 1963) helped me to understand the problem. Wilson classifies the family that live in estates such as Niddrie into three distinct types. He calls the families that can cope with the impact of life, events and values from outside the family 'The Solids'. He calls the families that cannot cope 'The Difficults'. The third group, however, is by far the most interesting—'The Brittles':

'These are families which present the outward appearance and, usually indeed, the reality of maintaining conventional standards, but in which enormous effort goes into the appearances, maintained only at the expense of internal anxiety, distortion of strong natural feelings in order to conform, and, possibly, the playing of roles or refusal to be natural in ways which can be borne only with difficulty by spouses and children. These families tend to be found among the socially ambitious, on the one hand, and the socially overawed, on the other; or among those where one spouse has to carry the distorted personality of the other'. (*op. cit.*, pp. 16ff)

'The Brittles' then, are families which tend to draw the veil over lives which are flawed or unstable. In their desire to appear to be 'Solids' they take the leadership in social or community groups:

'We wrote earlier of the "Martyrdom complex" of the elected officers in a voluntary association. . . We may then see that their apparently curious behaviour is based on important reasons of which they themselves are in fact unconscious. For some, community life is a retreat from responsibilities in the home or from stresses and strains which are felt to be unbearable. For others, it may help to compensate for lack of prestige at work'. *Stress and Release in an Urban Estate*, (John Spencer, p.55; Tavistock Publications, 1964)

Community Associations, therefore, appeared to occupy a high proportion of the time of 'The Brittles', a group which Norman Dennis (in 'The Popularity of the Neighbourhood Community Idea', *The Sociological Review*, V1.2, December, 1958) calls 'the troublemakers'. Unfortunately, they did not simply confine their attentions to community efforts. In Niddrie 'The Brittles' were very much in evidence within the church.

Richmond Craigmillar, of course, included a good number of 'solid' families within the congregation. However, very few 'difficult' families had found their way into the church. The chief obstacle appeared to be 'The Brittles'. These families, insecure and frightened, clung to the church for support. They were the ones to emphasise the traditional nature of the church. They wanted Richmond Craigmillar to be like St Giles, or at least similar to the Old Church in West Richmond Street prior to its transportation*. Because they were afraid of the 'animals' in their own stair, they showed a marked disinclination to receive them into their church, the last citadel of safety in a parish full of 'difficult' families. They spoke of the church as being their 'spiritual home' and they desperately wished that it could provide them with the security which their own homes lacked. Although a distinct minority within the church, they had often assumed places of leadership within the congregation. For this reason, their opinions often carried great force. Their vehement denunciations of change which they made at Session and congregational meetings often spelled out their own need for defence in the midst of a world which appeared hostile and frightening to them.

It was all very well to understand the problem, however. It was much more difficult to find an

*A technical word in Church of Scotland vocabulary relating to the movement of a church and congregation to another place. See A. Herron, *A Guide to Congregational Affairs*. The Saint Andrew Press, 1978, pp. 91f.

answer to it. The teachings of Jesus of Nazareth were in direct contradiction to the needs of 'The Brittles'. Jesus had blessed the meek and the poor in spirit. He had sent his disciples out to greet them with the good news that the kingdom of God was at hand. This was too great a burden for the 'brittle' members of the congregation to bear. No matter how much they were directed to prayer and to Bible study, no matter how attentively they appeared to listen to the words of each sermon, in the end their private fears outweighed the impulse to love. For the moment, they could not become missionaries.

It remained true, however, that the church needed a lead in the direction of mission. The team decided to give that lead but to attempt to give it in a way which would not be frightening to the more 'brittle' members of the congregation. Our mission would take the form of a Summer church school.

Until the Summer of 1966, there had never been a Summer church school within the parish. There were good reasons for having one. Our Sunday School only attracted youngsters from the vicinity immediately adjacent to the church. There were large numbers of children, therefore, who had little contact with the gospel of Jesus Christ other than a religious service at school. Here was a field which was ripe for mission. Surely it would not prove too daunting for the congregation?

Ena Finlayson supervised the creation of the Summer church school. Douglas and I co-operated with her. We obtained the use of Niddrie school for the project so that we could teach in an environment to which many of the pupils would already be accustomed. Since it was situated at the opposite end of the parish, it was an ideal location.

Members of the teaching staff were readily recruited from the congregation. Some even donated their holiday-time for the project. Several volunteers from other Edinburgh churches assisted as well. It was decided that the best time for the Summer church school would be in the week immediately following the Trades' Fortnight. At this time many children were often found in Niddrie with little or nothing to do. Ena, in constructing the programme, made certain that the Summer church school would be a lively place to learn about Jesus Christ. Each morning it was planned to hold classes for children aged five to fourteen from nine to twelve noon. The programme would be varied from day to day. After morning worship, a film might be shown or an opportunity given for discussion. Then there would be classes from the teachers who had rigorously prepared their assignments. After a break for orange juice, crisps and recreation, the children would be allowed to choose from a wide variety of crafts such as dramatics or map-making. In the afternoons, they could return for a general recreational programme or for visits to specific parts of the city.

There was brilliant sunshine on the first day. The staff assembled at half-past-eight. I peered up and down the streets. There were no children to be seen. Fifteen minutes later, however, the pavements were thronged with youngsters making their way to Niddrie School. They hadn't stayed in bed after all! Enrolment on Monday revealed that two hundred and fifty children had attended the school. We maintained that average throughout the rest of the week. The good weather held and it was reflected in the good spirits of all who participated. On the final Friday evening, fifty parents were interested enough in our efforts to come along and pay us a visit. There was no doubt in anyone's mind, that our first Summer church school had been a success.

Our Summer youth programme was now flourishing. On the one hand, we had been able to make the claims of Christ Jesus quite explicit to large numbers of children who had little experience of the Christian faith prior to the Summer church school. On the other hand, by making use of the cottage at Stow, we were able to explore group-structures already existing within the community and open up the way for faith to make its impact. However, the Summer would soon be coming to an end. What would happen to all of these young lives with whom we had made contact when Winter came? Would it be possible to achieve an element of continuity between the Summer youth programme and the life and work of Richmond Craigmillar parish church? Could the congregation continue to expand its missionary role within the parish?

From the beginning, our team had been aware of this problem. To help us to solve it, we had recruited two students from Moray House School of Community Studies: Tom Passmore and Danny Yarrow. Initially, the Director of the School had been sceptical about sending his students to help in a church. It had never been done in the past. I was certain, however, that Danny and Tom would find their experience in Niddrie extremely helpful for their future work. They would undoubtedly be helpful to us as well. In the end, the Director agreed.

One sight of Douglas was enough to convince him that this was a most unusual situation.

Danny and Tom came to live in Niddrie at the beginning of July. They were given lodgings with families in particularly difficult areas within the parish. During the Trades' fortnight, they were expected to familiarise themselves with the geography of the district. Then came the Summer church school. Both men supervised the recreation during the morning breaks. In the afternoons they met the youngsters again, taking them swimming, fishing or camping. Several times, they organised trips to specific points of interest: the Edinburgh Castle or a museum. They were very busy.

Danny and Tom were an instant success. They fitted in well with the families who gave them 'digs'. Danny stayed in Niddrie Mains Terrace. Tom, on the other hand, lodged with a 'difficult' family in Niddrie Marischal. The father of the house was unemployed; the mother was a drug addict and sleeping with her husband's brother. Her own brother, recently out of prison, was inclined to get drunk and brandish a knife. Besides these people, the household also included three children, a large dog and Tom. Undoubtedly, the young student learned more about the life of a 'difficult' family from the people in his 'digs' than from all the books that he might have been able to read at Moray House.

Although they won acceptance from the children, older residents were inclined to be more apprehensive. Who were these strangers? What did they want? The question of identity was a difficult one. One dark night Tom was approached by a group of young men as he walked back to his 'digs':

'What are you doin' here in Niddrie?' asked their leader, a tall young fellow with long hair hanging down over his face. Tom, puzzled, decided to tell the simple truth: 'I work for Mr Christman', he replied. That was enough for his Interrogator.

'You work for that ***** minister', he shouted and threw himself on Tom.

As they rolled on the ground, Tom knew that he was surrounded by the rest of the gang. His present task, however, occupied all of his attention. At last, he flung the fellow to the pavement. Placing his foot over the lad's mouth, he spoke for the first time since the beginning of the fight:

'What did you say?'

The young man mumbled and then was silent. Tom looked around. He was encircled by the gang. There was a tense moment. Then the boys began to laugh—not at Tom but at the lad beneath his boot. They were still laughing as Tom walked away, leaving his adversary behind in the night.

Such incidents were few, however. On the whole, the students experienced little difficulty. By the end of their first month, they strolled the streets of Niddrie to the sound of shouted greetings and waving hands. Excursion after excursion was made to the cottage at Stow. They made contacts with hundreds of children and, as the Summer progressed, they concentrated on the small groups with which they had gained the greater amount of acceptance.

The end of the Summer brought with it the problem of continuity. Some of the work of transition was handled by members of the team. Each one of us had become involved with at least one group at the cottage in Stow. We intended to keep this work going. There were other ways that the team could be helpful, to be sure. The groups of young people with whom our Summer students had been involved had to be catered for as well. This was a very delicate process. Children attracted by Danny's personality, for instance, might not be so easily drawn to another. Although the spadework for transition was carefully done, it was not always successful. In fact, several groups simply fell apart with the departure of Danny and Tom. Most remained, however. Tom, for instance, had gathered together a group of young boys who wanted to play football. With the help of Douglas Templeton, he was able to introduce the boys to a manager and a trainer. Suddenly, he was no longer needed. The group was able to make progress without him. A discotheque begun by Danny was handled in a similar fashion. On the other hand, members of the church were involved in the process of transition as well. Every member of the Summer church school was contacted at the beginning of the Sunday school term, often by a teacher with whom he was familiar. The result was a growing Sunday school. Out of the experiences with the children during the recreational breaks, a youth club for children aged nine to eleven was devised. Church members were recruited to become its leaders. It was housed in the hall at Niddrie school.

The result of these activities was a youth programme which was quite extensive. Eventually, during the Winter months, it included five football teams, a folk-singing club and three swimming clubs. An expanded Sunday school and the youth club at Niddrie school were direct results of the Summer church programme. There were also the various *ad hoc* groups of youngsters which met with members of the team regularly each week. Most of these groups and clubs grew up separate and apart from the more traditional organisations which were located in the church hall. Because they had come about as the result of conversations in the closes and walks through the streets, they were not governed by specific rules and regulations. As a result, the church found them difficult to categorise, difficult to understand. They only corresponded to the logic of this particular parish, this particular community.

How was it possible to bear a missionary witness to these various groups and organisations? Within the Sunday school or the Summer church school, there was no problem. In these groups, a place had been made to speak about the gospel. The activities revolved around Bible studies. The young people who came along accepted this. They were ready to listen and to try to understand. It was more difficult to be a missionary within the context of a youth club or within a football team. Most of the young people who came along to these activities were from 'difficult' homes. It was not easy to cope with them. No wonder that many 'brittles' simply shrugged their shoulders and dismissed them as 'animals'. 'Christ died for everybody'—but not for them. . . .

What was the best way to take the good news of the gospel to these young people? Soap-box oratory had no appeal for them. They were not hostile to it. It was simply that words had no motivating force in their lives. Speeches could not reach them, these young people educated on comic books and television commercials. If words could not deliver the message of Jesus Christ, however, perhaps our lives would. If every committed Christian in the church could invest his life in service of others in the parish, perhaps the point would be made. Over the years, it was apparent that sometimes this did happen. Generally, it would be signalled by a question. A young lad might draw me away from a group of boys:

'How can you be bothered with us? Don't you know they're makin' a mug of you. Why do you do it?'

Answers would rarely be expected. The best answer of all was the cross of Jesus Christ.

Once I saw a boy of seven playing with a rubber ball in Niddrie Mains Terrace. He was dressed in rags. His face and hands were dirty. He had never known his father, his mother was a prostitute, but he had a rubber ball to bring him happiness in Niddrie Mains Terrace. Out of the close across the street burst a screaming child of the same age dragging his mother behind. He pointed to the lad with the rubber ball. Shouting at the top of her lungs, the woman crossed the road, snatched the ball and returned triumphantly to her own home, taking her smirking boy with her. The lad without his ball was left alone, standing with anguish showing upon his pinched and grubby face.

The place for cross-bearing disciples of Christ in Niddrie was to stand beside such children in their distress. Because it cost them so much, most people in the church could not do it. Until they learned that words were cheap but lives were valuable, they could never become missionaries to the people of their parish. They had to learn to become 'mugs' before they could become missionaries.

CHAPTER ELEVEN

An Excerpt from my Diary

It is Friday, 12 August 1966. I have decided to take Professor Cheyne's advice; I will keep a diary. Today has been an ordinary Summer's day. It is as good a place to begin as any other.

I wake about seven in the morning. I have to get up early because I am a host. Last night, when I returned to the manse, I found two social workers and a group of teenagers from London waiting for me. I knew one of the workers slightly. He asked me if I could give the group overnight accommodation. After finding beds and sofas for them, I went to sleep. That was 1 a.m. I am still tired.

While the group is in the kitchen preparing breakfast, an elder calls by the house. He says that he is worried about his relationship with the church. His new job makes regular attendance at the morning worship service very difficult since he has regular Sunday employment. He also asks to use my typewriter to write a message for his wife. Then he goes away.

The group goes away, too. As I am waving them 'goodbye', the telephone rings. It is an American tourist. His father painted my father's house. We therefore have a close bond of fellowship. Will I show him around Edinburgh? I meet him and his friend at a central coffee-house. After our conversation, I only have time to give them some advice and some maps of Edinburgh. My time is not my own!

I have lunch with Professor Cheyne, and he then suggested that I begin this diary. Afterwards I immediately go to visit the Royal Infirmary; I have four patients to visit there. However, when I arrive, I find that they have all been returned home. I have visited two in the past. I should have visited the other two at the beginning of last week when I first learned that they were ill. But—too little time. Douglas and Ena are away on holiday so I run the whole show myself.

I drive back to the manse and attempt to catch an hour's sleep. No luck! Danny rings the bell. He has come for his living expenses. Thanks to a grant from the Home Board, I can provide them. He'll take Tom's to him as well. We have a good talk over coffee. Danny would like to work with us again next Summer. He would also consider working part-time in Niddrie. We could use him. But where is the money to come from? We shall see.

I miss my evening meal because Davy and Dul call by the manse unexpectedly. It is good to see them. We go along to the movies and, afterwards, make a few plans about the future of our group. I leave them in Niddrie and get back home about 11 p.m. I am just opening the door when a young fellow staggers out of the park across the road. His face is cut and his nose is bleeding badly. He tells me that he is an epileptic and that he has been beaten up by a group of lads who despise him for his weakness. After I tidy him up, I drive him home to Niddrie. On the way back, I see a lad staggering along the road. It is Don, an unemployed teenager who is drunk. I take him back to his home as well. Then at last I get back to my own bed. The time is 1 a.m. Again.

Afterthought:

This was the first and only time that I found the opportunity to write a page for my diary. The church lost contact with the elder eventually. Evidently his new employment made participation at either worship service impossible. I lost contact with the London social workers, too. However, I did see the epileptic lad and Don quite often. They always wrote to me to ask for a visit whenever they happened to land in prison.

CHAPTER TWELVE

Dead Wood or Kindling?

At the time of my induction, an article appeared in *The Edinburgh Evening News*. It stated that I was eager to 'put on my walking shoes and hike round the parish'. One year later, I was still hiking.

It had seemed to me that one of the best ways of revitalising the congregation of Richmond Craigmillar was to visit personally every member of the church. Easier said than done! For one thing, it was difficult to find a time when I could make a visit. Mornings and afternoons were suitable for visiting old and sick people and the shut-ins. Only in the evenings, however, could I have a fair hope of finding a family at home. On the other hand, it was only at night that our various adult organisations could meet. Through the lack of a choir master, I found myself leading the singing of the choir. Kirk Session and Congregational Board meetings occupied additional evenings. The 'vestry hour' occupied the whole of Wednesday nights. Other evenings were filled by talks to the Woman's Guild, appearances at church organisations, money-raising speeches given all over the city and the occasional lecture at an evening class at New College.

All of these activities filled my nights, from Monday to Thursday. On Friday night, the church

103

was dead. Traditionally, it was Dad's night out, while Mother waited in the house to pay the bills. No-one, therefore, could reasonably expect any adult to come along to the Kirk on a Friday evening. Any money left in Dad's pocket after Friday was usually spent by Mum and Dad on Saturday night. Another night's entertainment: no-one in the Church. Sunday evening was different. With their money spent and the local pubs closed, Mum and Dad usually stayed at home and watched the television. They needed a quiet night to recover from their respective hangovers. Of course, they wouldn't consider coming near the church on these weekend evenings. They didn't welcome a visit from the parish minister either.

Occasionally on a Saturday night, when my sermon preparation was finished and the manse was quiet, I felt twinges of self-pity. The pubs in Niddrie were full of merriment. The Miners' Social Club would be packed. Yet I stood outside of all this. I had no family in the district and I knew that the presence of a minister would be scarcely welcome in the lounge bar of the local. A girl-friend would have been comforting. But how could I find one? If I asked a local girl out for the evening, tongues would be certain to wag. We had enough gossip in the church already! On the other hand, I never received invitations to social functions in any other part of the city. It was a difficult problem.

But, although these weekend evenings were usually quiet for me, Sunday more than compensated. In the morning, I usually conducted the worship service. Some afternoons, I assisted with the Boys' Brigade. However, I preferred to have the time to think about the evening service at which I also preached. Afterwards, I might take a new communicants' class, speak at the youth fellowship, lead a meeting of our newly formed young adults group or give a talk at one of the numerous youth groups throughout the city.

It was a busy week, with little time for myself. Nevertheless, there were some nights when I had no previous appointment. No organisation needed me. Almost always, however, there were people who did. There were young families to visit in regard to the baptism of their children; young couples to interview about their intended marriage; widows to console prior to the funerals of their husbands. Usually these men and women were not members of the church. The congregation began to feel slighted.

'He was in my stair', said one old woman to Ena, referring to my activities 'but he didn't come to see me.'

Hers was a common complaint. In order to answer it, I redoubled my efforts at visitation. The elders, seeing that I was growing tired, extracted a promise from me that I would take a day off. It was a promise which was impossible to fulfil. The most that I could manage was to take the occasional Friday evening off, since the people of the parish were not anxious to see me then anyhow.

Occasionally, there would be hours or evenings when, by sheer hard work, I was able to create time for pastoral visitation to the members of the Congregation. When these opportunities occurred, I was prepared to make use of them. Armed with lists of church members, I trudged up and down the dimly-lit streets of Niddrie, knocking on the doors of all whose names appeared on the congregational roll. I discovered that there were three types of visitation required. The first was to the church regulars. A visit from the deaconess or the assistant was not enough for these people; they demanded a visit from their minister. It was their right: They came to Church. The father might be a member of the Congregational Board; the mother a member of the Woman's Guild. The children would attend the Sunday school faithfully. I recognised their faces easily. They demanded attention because they were pillars of the church. I was quite willing to give them that attention. Some times, however, I did wonder what we really had to say to one another during the course of these visits. We saw each other regularly each week in the church anyhow.

Another type of visit was necessary to those families who felt a strong attachment to the church but who, for one reason or another, were not able to come along regularly. In these houses, my visits were greeted with embarrassment and excuses. Many of them were young couples struggling to bring up their children properly in a difficult environment. If the father was a responsible fellow, he was probably working overtime in order to save the money to take his loved ones out of Niddrie. Mother, on the other hand, would be preoccupied with the business of child-raising. Often her sitting-room would be festooned with drying nappies. These were the people who had the ability to create a new type of church, but they would never do so. They were quite content to confine their interests to their own needs and to hope for a better tomorrow when they could move away. Once they had made their move, they would no doubt become participating members of the church which they continued to ignore in Niddrie.

The great majority of the congregation, however, fell into neither of these two categories. These were people unknown to me, the faces of strangers which would appear every now and then at a communion service. My visits to these families varied in their nature. Some of them were argumentative. Others were demanding. Most, however, were utterly indifferent to the church. Why they bothered to remain church members puzzled me. One man described his membership as a kind of religious insurance policy, 'Just in case there might be something up there'.

Typical was the interview which I had with a middle-aged couple who lived one block away from Richmond Craigmillar. It was a wild night, the rain was pouring down. Since my car was in the garage for repairs, I was on foot. When I had located the address that I was seeking, I stepped inside the stair for shelter and searched for the couple's door in the dim light. My notes indicated that both husband and wife were members of the church and that they had attended communion eighteen months before. I knocked at the door, and then knocked again. Listening intently, I could hear the sound of voices. No one answered. I went back down the steps and outside into the driving rain. I could see that a light was burning in the couple's sitting-room. It was possible, of course, that they had left the television and lights on in order to keep away burglars. There was still a chance, however, that they might be at home. Again I knocked at the door, this time with all my strength. There was a moment's hesitation and then some sign of response. Eventually the door opened. In the passageway stood a middle-aged woman, short, stout with hair that was in the process of turning white. She grunted and, without further comment, turned back into the house, leaving the door open behind her. I interpreted this to be a welcome and followed her into the sitting-room, after closing the door behind me. The man of the house was watching television. He glanced at me, nodded and resumed his concentration. I sat down and attempted a conversation. In return, I received a bit of dialogue from 'Coronation Street'.

'Would it be possible to turn the sound down a bit', I suggested.

Husband and wife glanced at one another. The woman rose to adjust the set, with little noticeable effect on the volume. Again I tried a conversation— the weather, taxes, anything that I could think to say. Eventually, I asked them about the church. The communion roll indicated that it had been eighteen months since they last attended a communion service. Had someone been ill? Was anything keeping them from attending the church? The woman's face brightened. Now she knew why I had come. Previously she had been puzzled about my motives. Perhaps I had been going to ask for money. Reassuringly, she declared that she would try to come to the church on the following Sunday. As for her man, she said, he wasn't much of a church-goer. In fact, he never came at all. She took along his communion card with her whenever she happened to be going to the communion service. When I chided her a bit for this practice, she sank back into silence.

I was overcome with a feeling of helplessness and rose to leave.

'Oh no', she said, 'You can't go without a cup of tea'.

Defeated, I sat down again. I waited in silence while the kettle slowly boiled and one television programme succeeded another. Having endured the ritual of tea and biscuits, I made my excuses and left. As I hurried down the stairs, I wondered if I would have the time to make another congregational visit before the night was over. . . .

Such experiences were typical as I made my way from door to door. In vain did I look for the fruits of such labours to appear on a Sunday morning. They were simply not to be found. The pews still remained half-empty. After two years devotion to such pastoral visitations, I was completely disillusioned. Most members of the congregation that I visited appeared completely immune to the call of the gospel, their responsibilities to the Kirk, or to the demands of common courtesy. Although I had not expected them all to flock to the church, the records indicated that whether they had been visited once, twice or even more times by the minister, the assistant minister or the deaconess, the result was the same: No Sale! These people were the dead wood in our congregation. If my hope was to build a more vital church which believed and worshipped and served, the presence of these men and women could only act as a deterrent to others who had come into the church believing that their statement of faith was the turning-point in their lives. For these reasons, I decided to initiate a purge of the congregational roll.

The Kirk Session had been eager for the roll to be purged. As the elders visited their districts, they returned to Session meetings with tales of members who had told them that they 'could not be bothered about the Church'. Some elders complained that members would not allow them into their homes. Indifference seemed to be the chief characteristic of the congregation at Richmond Craigmillar.

We began by purging those members whom we could not locate. There were a number of these people. Some had emigrated; some had been lost as they moved away from the parish. In Niddrie, however, there was the peculiar problem of 'the moonlight flit'. A 'moonlight' was undertaken by families about to be evicted in order to preserve their few personal belongings from sale at the hands of the Sheriff's Officer. Often on an evening these people could be seen pushing prams full of goods along the streets of Niddrie under cover of darkness. We placed all of these people—about eighty in number—on the supplementary roll. It was the first time that a supplementary roll had been created in my parish.

However, when we approached the congregation which remained, we experienced greater difficulty. The Session decided that only if a member had not attended a communion for three years would he be eligible to be placed beside the 'lost brethren' on the supplementary roll. But were all members to be treated in this fashion? What about the man who never came to church but who sent his donation in regularly? What about the woman who was never to be found at communion but who attended the old time dancing class? What about the husband of the faithful Guild member who was never present himself at the Kirk? What about the waitress who worked regularly on a Sunday and who could never therefore attend communion?

All of these matters were immediately raised by our elders at the Kirk Session meeting which considered the purging of the roll. It was agreed that no one who was ill or elderly should be struck from the communion register. I found it surprising, however, that these elders, who had seemed so very keen to revise the roll, should now attempt to find excuses for most of the cases which were placed before us! If we struck one member off of the roll, we would offend his wife. If we struck another member off, we would lose his donations. So the story went. In the end, the Session decided to take action in only one hundred cases, less than one-third of our indifferent members. These people were to be sent letters of warning. They must attend the next communion or risk the loss of their membership. I agreed to visit all of the members cited in this fashion. The eventual outcome was that almost all of these men and women did come along on the following Communion Sunday. Only thirty names were struck from the list of communicants. However, having made this effort, the members fell at once back into their old habits. It did not require a gift of prophecy to realise that, in three years, the whole process would have to be repeated once again.

Why didn't these people want to come to the church? Perhaps the fault lay with me, with my approach during visitation or with the type of sermon which I preached in Richmond Craigmillar. Perhaps they just didn't like my personality. Perhaps the answer to the problem was to be found in the history of Scotland where for centuries working-people had been provided with Kirks which were maintained for them. Perhaps at the end of the day, the local community did not really need or desire a church in which to worship. I recalled Hugh Miller:

'Demand and supply were admirably well balanced in the village of Niddry: there was no religious instruction and no wish or desire for it'. (*op. cit.*, p.323)

Wherever the fault lay, the fact remained that the majority of the members of Richmond Craigmillar were indifferent to the claims of Christ Jesus and of his Church. They were dead wood. About this time, I was invited to preach at a small Baptist church in Dalkeith. The contrast between the two churches interested me greatly. Dalkeith Baptist church was a small congregation with only one hundred and twenty members on the roll. It was obvious from the attendance at Sunday morning worship that most of these members came to the church. These people also provided the membership for the various organisations which met during the week. Certainly, Dalkeith couldn't be compared with Niddrie in terms of social deprivation—and the social problems were the factors which often conspired to keep the Niddrie folk from fulfilling their responsibilities to the Kirk. Yet the small lively congregation in Dalkeith provided us all in Niddrie with an example for our guidance.

This was the type of church which I had hoped to build in Niddrie. I had every opportunity to do so. Young people were flocking to the new communicants' classes, families were bringing their children to be baptised and the impact of the church upon the local community was growing daily. I had been badly shaken by my failure to lift the indifference which was characteristic of the greater part of the congregation. There were other failures as well. The first class in adult Christian education failed to attract half-a-dozen members. Our young wives' group collapsed when it was discovered that all of the young wives were about to become young mothers at approximately the same time. All the same, the church appeared to be succeeding in its missionary work. Since many hearts within the established congregation appeared to be indifferent to the gospel of Jesus Christ, we would need to build our revitalised church with the help of those who were now coming into it. The way for Richmond Craigmillar appeared to lie with those who, until recently, had been 'outside the camp'. With this in mind, I decided to direct a good deal of my attention to these 'new recruits'.

CHAPTER THIRTEEN

For Services Rendered

It was traditional to hold a Christmas Eve service at Richmond Craigmillar. The church was packed for the occasion. Extra chairs had to be brought in to seat the congregation. Old and young alike could be seen making their way to the church. Many were familiar faces, members of Richmond Craigmillar. Others, however, were strangers to me, drawn to the church by the Christmas spirit. Some indeed, had been partaking of the Christmas spirit since the pubs opened at five in the afternoon! They would stagger into the church, drop their heads between their knees and be sick. A few occasionally would try to start a fight. No wonder that I looked forward to these Christmas Eve services with dread.

Christmas Eve 1966 proved particularly difficult. At the beginning of the service, five young men were ushered to seats at the front of the church, directly below the pulpit. They were very drunk. At this point, the large congregation rose to sing the first Christmas hymn. In the last verse was a reference to the Virgin Mary.

'Virgins!' exclaimed one of the drunks, as the congregation took their seats, 'That reminds me of a story.'

In a loud voice, he told a dirty joke. Behind him,

many of the older members of the church were annoyed.

'Shush', said one old age pensioner, 'That's not nice'.

The men were undismayed. 'I can tell a better one than that', said one. He proceeded to tell a really filthy joke about virgins.

During this time, I had attempted a prayer and a scripture reading. My voice, however, was drowned out by the ribald remarks of the men. From the back of the church came shouts as well:

'Throw them out', screamed one woman.

'Get them out of here', shouted another.

The congregation murmured its assent to these proposals.

I tried in vain to get the men to be quiet. I altered the sermon to speak about Aberfan. Surely no one could laugh at Aberfan! These men could, however. I addressed the men directly:

'You'll need to be quiet'.

'Certainly, Father' 'Sorry, Father'

More dirty jokes.

By this time, many people in the congregation were hurling abuse at the drunks who remained completely oblivious to the distress which they were causing. The scene was the antithesis of the spirit of Christmas and brotherly love. Finally one of the worshippers arose from his seat. He was a policeman. Stepping forward, he escorted the five drunks from the church. They went peacefully. Fifteen minutes later, the service was finished. I was shattered.

Later I attempted to locate the five men who had made the Christmas Eve service into such a shambles. No-one could tell me much about them. I did learn, however, that five days after Christmas, one of the men had committed suicide. Had he come to the church looking for help? I would never know.

I was asked to do many special services over the years at Richmond Craigmillar. A number of these were marriage services. I quickly learned that a marriage in contemporary language was not appreciated in Niddrie. These people wanted to 'get done' properly. Only the language of the *Book of Common Order* could convince them that they had been properly married.

It was difficult to capture the attention of the congregation during these marriage services. Occasionally a bird, for instance, would become trapped within the building. I could follow the eyes of the congregation as the bird would flutter from one end of the sanctuary to the other. I felt as if I had been sentenced to preach to an audience at Wimbledon, while the eyes of the people were intent upon the tennis ball.

One such service presented particular difficulties. The young couple were in the process of being married. They stood, together with the best man and best maid, at the front of the church with their backs to the congregation. It was a lovely Summer's day. All of the windows were open. Suddenly, into the church strode the bride's neighbour, an old woman with a notorious past. She was followed closely by her three illegitimate children. Puffing from the exertion, she lowered her ponderous frame into the first seat available. Her children surrounded her. Into the window nearest to where she sat appeared three boys. They began to chant rude slogans to the woman, reminding her of her past. She would not tolerate this sort of abuse! Her face flushed with anger, she made some loud remarks about the parentage of the lads and slammed the window loudly shut in their faces. She had hardly regained her seat when the lads appeared at the next window. Again the woman retaliated. During this time, a look of frozen horror had appeared on the face of the bride. Neither she nor the groom could see what was happening. But they did hear the slamming windows and loud obscenities which punctuated the remainder of the wedding service. As the bride and groom left the church, the neighbour stepped forward.

'I couldn't stay away', she said.

A look from the bride told her that her presence had not been entirely appreciated.

Funeral services were not generally conducted in the church, this honour being reserved for elders who had died. Generally, they took place at the crematorium. My first such service occurred at the Warriston crematorium, a cold and dismal place at the best of times. I was naturally very nervous. Because I was such a novice, I had decided to adhere to the funeral service set out in the Kirk's *Book of Common Order*. When it came time for the committal, I crossed over and stood behind the coffin. Since there was no lectern, I rested on the coffin. After beginning the appropriate sentence, I looked up to impress upon the congregation the importance of the message. I heard a gasp of surprise from a woman seated on the front row. Looking down, I had just enough presence of mind to snatch back my book from the coffin which was rapidly disappearing into the depths below. I never repeated that again.

In spite of these incidents, the response to these various worship services was heartening. One Wednesday evening, a young man walked into my Vestry.

'I've come to join the church', he said.

I was amazed.

'Do you want to get married or to have your baby baptised?' I asked. It never occurred to me that he might want to join the church without any prodding.

'I was at the funeral service which you took yesterday', he continued, 'I listened to the words which you read from the Bible. They seemed to be speaking directly to me. Now I want to become a member of your church'.

The man was sincere. He attended all the instruction classes and became a member of Richmond Craigmillar. Later, the Session asked him to become an elder.

On another vestry night, a young couple stepped into my office. They looked very trendy. He was a hairdresser and his wife was his assistant. They wanted me to baptise their little boy, although they did not live within the parish. I asked them why they had come to me.

'We were at the wedding which you took last Saturday', explained the man whose name was Charlie.

I explained to them the rules and regulations. Since they lived outside the parish, one of them would have to become a member of our church in order for me to be able to baptise the child. The couple listened in silence to what I had to say. They did not look offended but they rose to leave.

'That's all right. We understand', said Charlie, dismissing the idea of attending a new communicants' class as a waste of time. The next week he was back.

'When does that class begin? I'm ready to start'.

I asked him what had made him change his mind.

'My wife and I talked it over', he said, it all came down to this: I like your patter'.

Charlie Miller became a member of Richmond Craigmillar. For years afterwards, he attended the Wednesday night vestry. While I interviewed the people who had come for help, he helped them the best way that he could. He cut the hair of the men waiting to see me and gave their donations as a gift to the church. Whatever he might think about me, Charlie Miller was certainly no 'patter merchant'.

CHAPTER FOURTEEN

Help Wanted—and Found

I was sitting, waiting to be ushered into the office of the Editor of a leading Scottish newspaper. Several weeks before I had written to him asking for help. We needed help badly at Richmond Craigmillar. The various youth projects had gone remarkably well, but we did not have enough money to maintain them. Football teams needed their strip; youth clubs required equipment. Other groups such as the discotheque started by Danny also merited our attention. The church could not balance its own budget. It was in no position to offer assistance. As a result, I was forced to give money-raising talks throughout the city. The proceeds from these efforts—usually about five pounds—were hardly enough to keep the existing schemes going. It seemed a shame that work which was proving so successful should fail for lack of funds.

With this in mind, I had written to the Editor. My idea was that a Trust might be set up to provide the money necessary to support our many activities. I didn't know many influential men personally. For this reason, I had written to him to ask for advice in arranging the Trust and selecting the men to administer it. I opened by commenting on my letter. The more we talked, however, the more depressed I became. Although the Editor might have been interested in the project initially, it became obvious that he had no intention of helping us, even to the extent of recommending men with whom I might be in contact. Finally, I rose to my feet and thanked him for giving me the interview:

'When I wrote to you', I said, 'I figured that even if you refused to see me, I couldn't lose any more than the price of an envelope and a four-penny stamp'.

For a moment, the Editor fumbled in the top drawer of his desk.

'At least he's going to give me a donation', I thought, remembering that last week's 'take' from a talk to a Woman's Guild had not been very much.

The editor stretched out his hand. In it lay an envelope and a four-penny stamp.

'Now you haven't lost anything', he said.

It was a good thing for Richmond Craigmillar that many people were more co-operative than the Editor. The people who were most helpful, of course, were the members of our team.

After two years, it was time for Douglas Templeton to leave us. During the last few months of his ministry in Niddrie, he had become 'Dr Templeton' with the completion of his dissertation for the Ph.D. We were all very proud of him. However, we were even more proud of the work which he had accomplished in the parish. Although he was hardly the darling of the 'regulars' in the congregation, he was regarded as the friend of many 'difficult' families who lived within the parish. Beginning quietly, he had eventually achieved a position of stature within the community. His powers of persuasion within the Sheriff's Court were said to be phenomenal. Many a local lad had trained with him on the football pitch. Many a family had experienced his kindness and humility. He had accomplished a unique piece of work. He had lived where no Christian minister had lived before. He had exercised a truly pastoral ministry within the Niddrie community. He had made his progress from ridicule to respect. Now they all knew him: the pub-crawlers and prostitutes, the drug-addicts and the thieves. In his quiet and thoughtful way, he had given to many people a vision of a better life than they had ever encountered before.

Douglas left to become the chaplain at the University at Karlsruhe in Germany. I had to find a successor; I knew that this would not be an easy task. We needed a man for a new type of job. Douglas had worked almost exclusively within the community. As the result of his work, many people in the parish were looking at Richmond Craigmillar with a new respect. We were now searching for a man who could help to convert this respect into faith, a man who would feel at home in both the church and the community. It was a difficult job which could only be filled by a remarkable man.

I searched in vain. It seemed impossible to find a man with the sufficient abilities and maturity to undertake the work which was needed. Then someone mentioned that John Miller might be available to work in Niddrie. John Miller! The name conjured up a picture of a tall, fair man whom I had known at New College. I had always perceived him as something just a little less than Superman. Although I had been the Assistant Lecturer, his knowledge of classical languages had been far superior to mine. His game of Bridge was better too. If this man wanted to work in Niddrie, then I wanted him to come. Although some of the New College staff expressed doubts, I was certain that he could tackle any job. We met, discussed the work and, after ten days' consideration, John accepted. In a few days he had moved in with Mrs Forbes.

It didn't take long before people began to seek John's help. Douglas had opened the way. They came for football, for swimming, for counselling and for advice. He did not pretend to be another Douglas. He responded to their demands as a man with his own personality, his own values. Always his response was honest. As the months passed by, many people began to respect him as much as they had respected his predecessor. Their needs seemed to strike a note of response in John's character. His dedication never ceased to amaze me.

Within a year, he was married. His bride was Mary Robertson, a student of social work. He took her home to the flat which had been allocated to him by the corporation. It was in the centre of Niddrie. Soon it became a source of advice and consultation for the community at all hours of the day and night. It was not surprising that John's red eyes sometimes gave evidence of lack of sleep or that Mary occasionally answered an early morning phone call with a touch of acid in her voice. Both Mary and John wanted to continue to live within the parish, however. Neither wished to give up the opportunity to participate within the community.

We added others to our team as well. Each year, New College sent us a group of four or five divinity students for training. Our first group included a Welshman, an Irishman and three Scots. They gave us one evening per week. After a meal and a discussion, the boys would proceed with their field-work. Some began to visit the residents of the new high flats which had recently been erected on the perimeter of the parish. Others visited 'difficult' families in Niddrie Mains. The Irish lad helped us with the youth club which met on Thursday nights in Niddrie School. He was a big fellow, a rugby player, whose height and physique made him a 'marked man' at the club. The primary school boys delighted in wrestling with him. He would occasionally cuff one or another of them when their antics became too abusive. One night, he lost his temper with one eleven-year-old lad and struck him on the side of the face. The boy burst into tears.

'Just you wait. I'll tell my Big Sister.'

The Irishman laughed as the boy rushed off into the night. His face wreathed in smiles, he told me about the threat. As he was talking, I looked behind him. There stood not one but two of the most ferocious-looking women it had ever been my misfortune to encounter. They towered over the Irishman and were every bit as broadly built as he was. As he caught my eye, the rugby player turned. Seeing the women, his smiles vanished. Excuses followed:

'It was all a mistake. The boy just got in my way. I don't know how it happened.' All this as he backed off slowly.

It was the wee boy's turn to laugh as he left the playground triumphantly in the company of his two BIG sisters.

We had help from a host of volunteers as well. Moray House continued to send us Summer students for our youth programmes year after year. During the Winter months, we had helpers from the United States as well as from European countries such as Finland. Local people also gave us assistance. Some young men and women assisted in the youth clubs. Others helped in the Sunday school. Increasingly, a traffic was developing between the church and the community. People who were not members of the congregation still felt that the church was doing things that were worthwhile. They helped in a variety of ways.

One Saturday morning, for instance, I had asked the members of the congregation to come to the church in order to wash the walls of the sanctuary. At nine a.m., the scaffolding had been erected, the mops and buckets were ready, but only one lone elder had appeared to do the work. Together we mounted the scaffolding. It was extremely fragile. A false step would mean a long fall to the floor below. After half-an-hour, Davy, Dul and Harry appeared.

'What are you doing, Bill?' they asked.

'What does it look like I'm doing?' I replied, crossly.

The boys hung about the door of the church disconsolately. They had been hoping that we could all go for a swim.

'Do you want us to give you a hand?' asked Davy finally.

'Yeah. That would be great'.

All morning we worked on the walls. Eventually, we were joined by others. Some were members of the church. Others were friends of Davy, Dul and Harry. At last we came to a portion of the church which could not be reached from the scaffolding. The only way that it could be reached with soap and water was to swing out on a rope.

'I feel just like Tarzan', said one of the lads as, with mop in hand, he swung forward to finish the job.

What had begun as a task for church members had ended as an event in the life of the local community.

All of these helpers, however, required supervision. Divinity students, youth and community students and local volunteers all demanded time. In attempting to cope with the situation, the administrative abilities of the team were being stretched to the limit. The obvious answer was to employ a full-time worker to deal with the situation. The Home Board was approached. This time it turned a deaf ear. The cost of maintaining the team was already too expensive. The corporation could not help either. To help a church would set a dangerous precedent.

Eventually, however, there came an answer to our prayers. The Martin Trust generously agreed to donate £300 toward the salary of a full-time worker. It wasn't much, but it was a beginning. I approached the Community Service Volunteers organisation in order to find a man who would be willing to work with us for room, board and pocket-money. In quick succession, two fellows came and went. The first lad revealed a talent for laziness which would have rendered him unsuitable for any type of work, let alone the sort of energetic project which we had devised for him. One day his mother arrived from

England and lead him away to safety. The second volunteer was a gently soft-spoken fellow who was completely unequipped to deal with the demanding situation in Niddrie. When he arrived, he asked my permission to take one afternoon off per week in order to visit his psychiatrist. One day I was asked to pay a visit to the psychiatrist as well. He asked me to relieve the lad of his duties in Niddrie as soon as possible. Otherwise, he might soon suffer a nervous breakdown.

With half of our £300 spent, it was still apparent that the team was being overworked. We decided, therefore, to use the rest of the money to pay for the living expenses of an American divinity student. Perhaps he could become the full-time worker which we needed so badly. Soon it became clear that we had made another mistake. Our 'worker' simply wasn't doing any work. He had moved into the room made vacant by John's departure. As far as we could tell, he never went outside the door. Finally, in exasperation, I confronted him with our dissatisfaction.

'I don't like to go out in the rain', he replied.

With the termination of his employment, our £300 was exhausted. Still we had not found the help that we needed so badly.

We did receive help from an unexpected source, however. For some time, I had been considering what type of mission service might draw young people in the parish to Sunday morning worship. At last I thought that I had found the answer. One evening, I knocked at the door of Alan Anderson, captain of the Heart of Midlothian Football Club. He and his parents were charming, although I was a complete stranger to them. Later in the evening, I spoke to him about my idea. I was hoping to have a service of worship at Richmond Craigmillar which would bring many new young faces to the church. I needed a speaker. Would he be willing to come along and to give a talk about his understanding of the Christian faith? Alan's face was a picture of bewilderment. He said he wasn't a very good Christian. Furthermore, he didn't relish the idea of delivering an address from the pulpit. As we talked, however, he began to accept the idea. I maintained that it was important that a man with his position in the world of young people should be seen to stand up for the Christian faith. In the end he agreed to do it, provided that no reporter should be present to give him a red face in the next morning's headlines.

Alan came and he spoke well. Although the elders, with their customary bluntness, told him that his football club was playing rubbish, his presence in the pulpit attracted several dozen youngsters who, normally, would not have come to worship. Alan's address was brief, honest and very much to the point. What was more important was that young people in the parish should understand that Alan Anderson was a Christian who was not afraid to speak about his faith from the pulpit of a church. He was succeeded in the following years by other football players who came to give their witness to Jesus Christ. John Greig, the captain of Rangers, was the next speaker at our youth mission service. His address was well worked out and, in places even eloquent. Afterwards, over one hundred youngsters came forward to speak to John. Finally, Ronnie Simpson of Celtic came. No-one in the congregation could fail to be moved by his humility, his integrity and his rough humour. If this was a man to admire on the football pitch, this was also a man to respect in the pulpit. This time, the church was packed for the mission service. For an hour afterwards, Scotland's goalkeeper was kept busy signing autographs. And for each youngster, he had a special word of encouragement.

Any mention of the help which we had from the world of football would be incomplete without the name of Pat Stanton. Pat lived in the parish. His family, warm-hearted and kind, had often given me personal advice and support when I needed a helping hand. The Stantons were good Catholics. Pat, however, was always willing to help a local football team on its way to success. He didn't care whether the boys were Catholics or Protestants— and neither did I. He was equally willing to visit any boy who was sick in hospital.

One lad, thirteen years of age, was dying of leukaemia. Pat, knowing the situation, invited him to visit his home and to have a cup of tea. The boy walked back to his house in Niddrie Marischal afterwards, his pocket full of Hibs souvenirs. Several weeks later, he was taken into the Royal Infirmary. Hoping to cheer him up, I made arrangements for Pat to accompany me on my next visit. On the morning that we planned to go to the Royal, I telephoned the Hospital to ask about the boy's health. The nurse told me that he had been restless during the night. She was afraid that a visit from the Hibs Captain might prove to be too exciting for him.

I knew that the lad would be badly disappointed. After cancelling the visit with Pat, I took out the money in my pocket. There was one pound and a few shillings. I spent it on sweets and fruit. Perhaps it would help to compensate for Pat's absence. When I arrived in the Hospital Ward, I asked the Nurse for help:

'Where's the lad, then?' She said, 'Didn't they tell you? He had a bad night, and two hours ago, he died.'

Never have I been so overcome with grief. Afraid to drive home by myself, I had to telephone a member of the team to come and collect me.

'He was too young to die', I expostulated.

'Laddie, no one is ever ready to die'.

We hadn't managed to find the full-time worker that we needed. But we did have plenty of help from one another when things got rough. Increasingly, too, we had assistance from students throughout the course of the year. More and more local volunteers were coming forward to aid us with our projects as well. Then there were the unexpected offers of help which made us grateful to the donors as well as to God. Perhaps a student might turn up and offer to become a Sunday school teacher, or a parcel of food might arrive from a Woman's Guild in the Borders. Maybe the morning post would bring a cheque for three pounds or a car draw up to the manse door with children's clothing for the needy. Although at times it appeared that our search for assistance was futile, in the end help always came. However unexpected its appearance might be, we were always grateful.

CHAPTER FIFTEEN

Teaching and Television

'Your predecessor was the chaplain to the local schools', remarked a member of the congregation.

It was evidently expected that I should do the same job. Early in my ministry, therefore, I went school-hunting. It wasn't easy. They were scattered all over the parish. When I had at last located one primary and one secondary, I realised that there was another school left for me to find. Seeing a large building on the Niddrie Mains Road, I assumed that this was the school which I was seeking. I marched in, ready to declare that I was the new school chaplain. Unfortunately, there was no one to greet me. Pacing up and down, I looked for some sign that might lead me to the appropriate authorities. There was no sound to betray a living presence. Suddenly I looked up and caught sight of a large black object slowly approaching me. It was a nun—wrong school! I beat a hasty retreat and went to search again for the remaining building.

Being a school chaplain was demanding work. Each primary school, for instance, demanded a different technique. Since there was no large hall at Niddrie School, it was necessary there to go from class to class to speak with the pupils. At Craigmillar Primary, on the other hand, it was possible to gather the boys and girls together into two groups for worship services. In both of these schools, Ena helped me by teaching the infants. At Niddrie Marischal secondary school, it was the custom to divide the pupils into four groups for religious services on successive days. At the beginning, I attempted to visit various classes in Niddrie Marischal as well, in order to give religious instruction. One morning I walked in to a class filled with forty fourteen year old boys. There was a substitute teacher. She was from India. I explained to her that I would be telling the boys a short story. She giggled. Did she wish to retire until I had finished? She giggled. And retired. I told my story. After fifteen minutes, there was no sign of the teacher. I sent a lad to fetch her. When he came back, he shrugged his shoulders. She had escaped! She could not be found. By this time, the boys were playing games in the aisles. Some were sitting on their desks. Others were grouped around the windows. The noise grew louder and louder. I tried threats. I tried persuasion. Neither worked to still the commotion. Finally, I had an idea:

'Hands up, all the boys who want to play football for a team.'

Every hand shot into the air.

'Right, back to your seats. The first boy that moves or talks will be dropped from the team.'

It worked. They remained motionless and soundless until the bell rang thirty minutes later. I never did encounter the substitute teacher again. However, I determined not to go from class to class at Niddrie Marischal. It was too dangerous! I confined my efforts to the services which I held in the school for the pupils. There were also the Christmas, Easter and end-of-term services which all of the schools held at Richmond Craigmillar.

I was, however, no teacher. I had no experience of practice teaching. I had never developed a curriculum for children of any age. Initially, I told the boys and girls Bible stories. They were not particularly impressed. Next I tried stories drawn from real life. These did not particularly excite them either. Finally, I adopted a suggestion from Professor Cheyne. I began to tell a series of stories based upon the life of a single missionary. They were told as a serial. One class, for instance, might end with David Livingstone about to be mauled by a savage lion. What would happen next? 'Tune in—same time, same station.' Most of the children did in fact 'tune in', to the extent that they were able to remember incidents from previous stories with a clarity that amazed me. I am afraid that David Livingstone and Johnny Weismuller often got a bit confused in the telling. But the children listened with great interest. For the older children at the secondary school, however, I made use of the words of pop songs and the details of contemporary newspaper stories. The success of these talks could be gauged by the fact that they were often repeated to families and friends. Occasionally an old granny might stop me in Niddrie Mains Terrace to tell me that she had enjoyed particularly the story which had been repeated to her. Whether the moral had been retained with the story, however, was another matter.

The reception which I received from these schools often helped to bolster my sagging morale. Sometimes at Craigmillar primary school, my stories at the worship service would be greeted by applause— a fact which never failed to dismay the headmaster. At Niddrie school, my appearance in a classroom would be met with cheering. No doubt the boys and girls were happy to know that the usual lessons were about to be suspended while I spoke to them about the perils of darkest Africa. At Niddrie Marischal, the pupils were older and more sophisticated. A murmur of voices might greet my appearance at a worship service but it was difficult to know whether this indicated scorn or approval. At any rate, it was good to be made so manifestly welcome in the schools. I felt that I was being given an excellent opportunity to relate the teachings of Jesus to the every-day lives of the boys and girls.

Other benefits came as a direct result of my work in the schools. I had encouraged the children to give me a wave whenever they saw me walking along the streets of Niddrie. Whenever possible, I would stop and speak with them. Soon it was not unusual to be greeted by two or three different groups of young-sters as I walked or drove through the housing estates. Cries of 'Mr Christman' followed me wherever I went. Parents would look at me sus-piciously.

'Who is that?' they would ask their children.

'That's the minister', would be the reply.

In this way, the children became my best helpers in the parish. Each one acted as a public relations officer. They were my links with their parents. In such a large parish, with such a large turnover in the population every year, it was obviously im-possible for me to visit each and every home. What was important was that each family should understand that the minister and the church took a genuine interest in their personal well-being. They could seek us out when they needed our help. Their children bore that message of care and love with them as they made their way homeward from school night after night. They had become agents of our missionary enterprise.

If I needed proof of the importance of my contact with the children in the parish, I found it at the time when I was asked to appear on television. One morning, I received a telephone call from the studios of Scottish Television. It was Nelson Gray. He asked me to speak on 'Late Call', a weekly series of late-night chats about the Christian faith. I hesitated. What possible good could come from giving seven five-minute talks on the television? If it was only for an ego trip, who needed it? Thinking the matter over, however, it occurred to me that these Late Call talks might be used to a missionary advantage within the parish. After all, they were viewed all over Scotland. They were theoretically available, therefore, to every householder in the community. The problem was that Late Call was not exactly the most popular television programme in Niddrie. Most people only watched it when it came on after the football on a Saturday night. How could I get the local people to switch it on?

The answer to the problem lay with the children. Once I had decided to appear on the programme, I notified the local headmasters, telling the dates when it would be screened. I 'plugged' these shows myself as I made my visits to the various schools. The children were encouraged to set aside the week of my Late Call appearances as a special time when they might be allowed to stay up late enough to watch the series. Many of them were excited. Mr Christman was going to appear on the television, their own T.V. star, so to speak! Undoubtedly there must have been parents who scoffed and sent their boys and girls to bed. However, on the nights when the series was being screened, more families than usual were awake in Niddrie in order to have a look at Late Call. It was the first time that many had seen the programme.

The title of the series was: Problems in the Parish. It dealt with the difficulties of young people and old people, of working people and unemployed people who lived in Niddrie. Although I did not go into detail regarding particular personalities, I mentioned several prominent features in parish life such as the local 'Chippie'. Each of the seven talks was designed to speak directly to my parishioners. Admittedly this was unfair to the many people from other parts of the nation. On the other hand, however, I hoped that these people would be able to see some similarities between our situation and the one in which they lived.

The talks were all to be filmed on one afternoon, several weeks prior to the date when they were to be screened. By the time that I drove up to the studio, my nerves had become a bit ragged. I was beginning to regret the fact that I had not written my script in advance. In order to retain an air of improvisation similar to that which I employed in our evening worship services, I had only outlined my talks. I hoped to have enough presence of mind to be able to 'flesh them out' as I addressed the camera.

Once in the studio, however, I found that I was extremely ill at ease. The cameramen were indifferent. The director appeared positively hostile. I guessed that he was not particularly happy with his assignment. I had watched a Late Call programme during the previous week. In it, the poor minister had been given a deep chair. As a result, the viewers saw only his double chin suspended immediately above his spindly shanks. I declined the offer of such a chair myself and insisted that I be allowed to sit behind a table. The Director agreed.

'We'll have a rehearsal', he said.

I began my first talk shakily.

'Cut', shouted the Director.

I wondered what had gone wrong. Perhaps my delivery was not sufficiently convincing. I remained seated behind the table with my hands buried in my lap.

'Get those hands up on the table', bawled the Director, 'The audience will wonder what you're doing with them, otherwise.' My hands shot to the top of the table and remained there rigidly for the duration of the seven talks.

When the series at last appeared on television, I was afraid to watch. All I could remember about my television experience was the sight of the cigarette butts hanging from the lips of the cameramen. I did not think that the talks could possibly fulfil the purpose for which I had designed them. They made an immediate impact in Niddrie, however. Dozens of men and women whom I had never met previously stopped me on the streets. Their children had insisted that they watch the whole series. To their surprise, they had been impressed.

'I didn't think I'd ever hear a minister talk good sense', said one old woman.

From the letters which I received from all over Scotland, I gathered that the talks had been relevant to other communities as well. I found these expressions of goodwill quite moving. The people of my parish would never allow me to have a 'big head', however. Boarding a late-night bus one evening, I sat down beside a fellow who was also travelling from the city centre to Niddrie. After five minutes, he turned round to stare at me.

'Aren't you the minister that was on the telly last week?', he asked.

Swelling with pride, I replied that I was. He scrutinised me carefully and then pronounced his verdict: 'You were a lot better-looking on the telly than you are in person.' Obviously I could never become a Pop Star.

As the years passed, I worked closely with the teachers in all three of the schools. If a child arrived in class without adequate shoes, we might co-operate to help the needy family. If a group of boys seemed to be heading for trouble, we might confer about the best way to turn them from delinquency. In Niddrie Marischal school, twelve lads were chosen every year by the headmaster on the basis of need. I arranged for local churches in Aberdeen and Inverness to give the boys a free holiday. The lads arrived back in Niddrie with glowing reports of the hospitality which they had received in the homes of these good people. There was always a volunteer with them to arrange activities. His expenses were met by the Church of Scotland. In these ways, and in many others, we worked together with the school-teachers in the best interests of the young people of the parish.

As they grew older, many of these young people became responsible members of the community. They found jobs, were married in the church and eventually settled in the district. The 'extended family' of granny, mother and daughter provided the foundation of the social structure of the community. The difference was that many of these units were now being affected by the Christian faith and the Christian church. There were some youngsters, of course, who left school to pursue lives of crime and indolence. These teenagers might be seen playing cards in a close on a sunny afternoon or sipping a pint in a 'local' on a rainy day. They prowled through the streets of the parish in groups of ten or twenty. Isolated from the social process because of imprisonment in the past or unemployment in the present, they were potentially dangerous. Fear was their best weapon. I knew them all, however, and was not afraid. Gone were the days when a teenage boy might be embarrassed to be seen talking to the minister. Conversation was now quite easy. It might be a chat about a court case or the possibility of a job. Whenever I could offer a helping hand in such situations, I did so. It was generally accepted—not as help from an institution or agency but as help from a friend whom they had accepted.

The more that I became drawn into the life of the local community, however, the more I felt a degree of tension in regard to my identity as a 'professional' in the area. Many of the professional people—the doctors, health visitors, social workers and teachers—adopted consciously a policy which main-

139

tained a distance between themselves and their clients. In this way, they sought to retain their ability to deal objectively with local situations. I was in a different position, however. I was not employed by the Local Authority. I was employed by the church, represented in Niddrie by a group of local people. Often the 'professionals' failed to understand this significant difference in our positions. For this reason, I initiated a series of luncheons at a hotel located just outside the district. These meals were for all the professional workers in the district. It was strictly understood that there were no agendas for these meetings. They were designed instead to give people a chance to get to know one another personally. They were a great success. Ministers chatted with nuns. Doctors swapped stories with social workers. In these ways, we began to have a better understanding of the roles which we played within the community. Better still, we began to be able to recognise the distinct personalities which often lay behind the profession. Unofficially, these meetings helped to give us all support for the different and demanding work which we all undertook within the context of the local community.

CHAPTER SIXTEEN

A Sense of Failure

'It is never a failure to be a failure at Richmond Craigmillar', Professor Cheyne had told me. How I remembered his words. I fought against them. It was not easy to accept the prospect of failure.

There were many reasons to hope for a better future for Richmond Craigmillar, many new signs of life. One might have compared the church to an ancient tree, barren and lonely, which suddenly begins to grow new branches. Now its battered trunk supported a great amount of life: fresh fruit, beautiful blossoms and singing birds. How can it support such a burden? If the trunk be rotten, how will it be able to bear the additional weight?

It had been my opinion that, if Richmond Craigmillar was to be able to support its missionary activities within the parish, it would need to be renewed itself. Bible studies, preaching and prayers were all undertaken with spiritual renewal in mind. There were social factors, however, which appeared to thwart its success. Time and time again, I was reminded that the Church was not only the Body of Christ but also a group of people responsive to social tensions and pressures. In the end, these pressures often dominated the life of the congregation more than the teachings of Jesus of Nazareth.

Originally, our missionary purpose had been directed out to the young people of the parish. As we took the message of Jesus Christ to the street-corners and closes of Niddrie, we hoped that the church cared about them, that they would want to become a part of its fellowship. Many did. Young people flocked to join the church. Each year between one hundred and one hundred and fifty people entered the new communicants' classes. No one was forced to come. In the first class, I even attempted to dissuade them from joining. I emphasised that only faith in Jesus Christ, a deep knowledge of his presence, could be the reason for becoming a member of the congregation. They stayed on and became members. Because we had known them in the schools, in the cottage at Stow and in the youth clubs, they now wished to become a part of the church. Yet, in one year's time, most of these young people would never be seen again. Why was this?

One reason was due to social pressures outside the control of the congregation. The church and the community were victims of the Edinburgh Corporation's housing policy. Once a young couple had married, they had to obtain a house. It was not easy. There was a long waiting-list for council houses:

'Current estimates of the waiting period between lodging an application and being allotted a house were two and a half years for a newly married couple, two and a quarter years for a couple with one child and five to six years for an old couple. Discouraging though these figures were, they compared favourably with those of a few years ago. It should perhaps be explained that applications are accepted only from persons employed in Edinburgh or resident in the city for at least three years (exceptions to this period being allowed for regular members of H.M. Forces and the Merchant Navy). A "points system" is in operation to ensure allocation of houses according to need. Because of the shortage no applications can be considered from people who already have a house which is not certified as over-crowded or insanitary, even though that house may be unsuitable for them on medical grounds or may be otherwise unattractive and they would dearly love to move'. (David Keir, *op. cit.*, p. 382)

Since our parish was composed entirely of corporation houses, the young couples were forced to find homes elsewhere until they qualified through the points system for a house in Niddrie. They might rent a room and kitchen in an older part of the city and bide their time. However, situated far from Niddrie, it would be difficult for them to attend the church. Since few would have cars, they would be dependant upon public transport. If they lived in Granton or Leith, for instance, they would find it impossible to arrive in time for the Sunday morning worship service. Inevitably, therefore, many of these young couples asked for their membership to be transferred to a church which was closer to them. It was right and proper for them to do so. It remained true, however, that they would not be able to contribute to the renewal of the church in Niddrie which we were hoping to achieve.

Eventually, however, some of our young people

might return to live in the parish. Since Niddrie had been called the ghetto of Edinburgh for a long time, there would need to be some compelling reason for them to accept a house in the vicinity. It might be that they wished to live close to their parents. Many young people sought out the support which they could find from the stable lives of the families they had left. The extended family was often a great help to them. On the other hand, some young people would be so desperate for a house that they would take the first one offered to them. They might be young families living in unsanitary or overcrowded conditions. Invariably they would be offered a house in my parish. Because of alcoholism, unemployment or other social problems, their families might not be able to give them support within the district. As a result, they would need to be able to survive on their own. Many found the going difficult. Young wives could be in tears within a week of moving into their new home. Vandals might have torn down their new fence or the garden might have been destroyed. Obscenities might have been written on their walls or their children threatened. Whether supported or unsupported within the community, however, all of these families had similar problems in regard to church attendance. They all had at least one young child. Many had more. Without children, they would never have been allocated enough points to obtain a corporation house. These babies kept their mothers fully occupied and their fathers busy working to provide their maintenance. They could not contribute much to the renewal of the parish church for these reasons.

Social pressures within the congregation did not

aid our renewal at Richmond Craigmillar either. There were some new members of the church, after all, who remained in the community. Some were older and already had their own houses allocated to them in the district. Other newly-weds stayed with their relations or were able—illegally—to sub-let a house within the district. Often, however, these new members became disillusioned with the church. As one elder put it:

'There is every effort to bring people into the church, but there is nothing to keep them here'.

Certainly there were plenty of organisations and activities connected with the congregation and open to all its members. The new members, however, were made to feel that they did not belong in the church. The attending congregation of Richmond Craigmillar had for some time been dominated by a dozen large families. Roger Wilson might have called some of these families 'brittle'. A single family, for instance, might produce an elder, a hall convener, the president of the Woman's Guild and the leader of the Brownies. This monopoly on positions of leadership within the church was quite easy to achieve. At one Annual General Meeting, for instance, a group of new members of the church asked that the retiring members of the Congregational Board, the Church's financial body, should step down for a year rather than be automatically re-elected as in years past. However, so few of these new members were willing to volunteer for the vacant positions that, in the end, the retiring members were recalled to their former posts. In this way, the fellowship of the church had become dominated by a self-perpetuating *clique*. Ever defensive, it resisted attempts to recruit new members to the church and was sharply critical of any attempt on the part of new members to assume positions of leadership within the congregation. In their terminology, these new men and women 'did not know the ways of the Church'. Translated, this meant that these 'outsiders' had yet to learn how to be a part of an inward-looking church.

Because they were not allowed to take a significant role in the affairs of the congregation, our new members had to confine their attentions to matters which were peripheral. They wanted to help to renew the church, but the way was not easy. Shortly after my induction I had asked the Congregational Board to form a social committee in order to provide functions where church members might be able to meet one another informally. For several years, the committee produced social occasions attended only by members of the Congregational Board and the Woman's Guild. Then one of our new elders, recently recruited to the congregation, became the convener of the committee. Immediately there was a change of emphasis. The committee organised a series of socials which became popular throughout the whole of the district. They were well organised and attractive to many young adults. Soon it became difficult to obtain tickets. With success, however, came the inevitable complaints: Too many 'outsiders' were coming to these social occasions. What had they done for the church? Some members of the congregation resented the fact that these socials were no longer their own private preserve. Sometimes they even found it impossible to obtain a ticket. They felt slighted. This was their church, after all. They washed its floors and raised its money. As a result, the activities of the social committee were debated in Session discussions and Congregational Board meetings. Although the convener of the committee undoubtedly made mistakes from time to time, it soon became apparent that it was the enlarged fellowship of the church which 'the establishment' so heartily resented.

Social factors outside the congregation and social pressures inside the church were combining to frustrate our hopes for renewal. Our leadership suffered as well. During my first two years at Richmond Craigmillar, I had managed to locate twenty men from the congregation who were able and willing to undertake the duties of eldership. Two years later, more than half of these men were no longer elders. Some had left the area. I could not blame them. They were men of ability. They cared for their wives and families. No doubt they wanted homes in stairs which were not filthy and streets without rubbish and broken glass. So they moved away to better districts. Others became disillusioned with the church. They had hoped to find a fellowship which echoed the teachings of Jesus. They found instead a *clique* which used gossip and innuendo as weapons to maintain its rights. They left behind them a vacuum in the leadership of the church which was difficult to fill. As these men shrugged their shoulders and turned away, their despair reached out like plague to those who were entering into the church for the first time.

It touched me as well, for I was growing tired. Little things indicated this to me. No longer could I laugh when I caught sight of the children pulling slates from the church roof. I was only too aware of the cost of their replacement. Increasingly, I lost patience with the man who would talk about the baptism of his children for thirty minutes before telling me that the real reason he had come to see me was to ask for a loan. Once I had been able to ignore the occasional giggle from a teenager during the evening worship service. Now it only took a smirk or a snigger to make me lose my temper. There were days when I could not force myself to leave the manse. With a half-hearted effort, I made excuses to the people who had expected to see me.

Why was this happening to me? I could think of a variety of reasons. First and foremost was the sheer burden of work. Most of my mornings began at 8 a.m. After correspondence, I would usually spend the rest of the mornings at the schools. Any free hours before lunch might be spent at court or looking for a job for an unemployed youth. After-noons were devoted to visiting hospitals. Evenings I visited homes or attended meetings. There were few alterations in this schedule. People advised me to take a regular 'day off'. Easier said than done! Most days I was needed somewhere by someone. My summer holidays were taken in August or September. Sometimes I used them to give talks to raise money for the youth projects of the church. Once, I even took a group of Niddrie boys to Spain. I was not renewing my strength.

Being single was no great help to me either, although there was no immediate prospect of remedying the situation. I lost contact with many of my university friends. I was simply too busy to see them, unless it was over a hurried meal in the city. Many times, however, meal-time was a fish-supper eaten on the way to the next meeting. I knew enough about the dangers of loneliness to take safeguards against becoming too emotionally involved in the lives of the people of Niddrie. They had enough troubles of their own! I wanted to be open and accessible to all of my parishioners. I didn't want any special relationship to block their way to me. When people told me that they attended the church because of my personality, I was genuinely upset. I wanted them to come for the right reason, because they believed in Jesus Christ as I did. Sometimes, however, I was lonely. There were nights when I could hardly bear to return to the cold and empty manse. How I wished for a warm fire and a cup of tea on those evenings! How I longed for someone with whom I might share the problems of the parish, someone who could understand without being directly involved! Yet there was no one.

My health also began to trouble me. I had been born in Joplin, Missouri—the 'Gateway to the Ozarks'. The Summers there were long and hot. I had not been prepared for weather which was often chill and damp, even in July! The roof of the manse leaked and several of the rooms were damp. Week after week found me with a bad cold or a case of the 'flu. Ena always advised me to stay in bed and look after myself. However, there were always visits to be made, baptismal services to conduct. Whether the other members of the team were available made no difference. The people demanded the presence of the minister in their homes and in their pulpit. So, in sickness or in health, I continued my work. Codeine tablets were used to kill the pains in my head, aspirins to lower my temperature. Eventually, of course, the chip suppers took their toll. My doctor warned me about the possibility of an ulcer. For a week, I tried milk puddings. Then I gave them up. It took too much time to prepare them.

Financial difficulties were never far away either. The minimum stipend might conceivably have been sufficient if I had been paid adequate expenses. There was no chance of that, however. The allowance which the church gave me for petrol never came close to paying for half the bills. The Bibles distributed at wedding ceremonies and the transport costs for football teams to various parts of the city could not be subsidised by the congregation either. I paid for them, believing that the church was in a worse financial situation than I was, if only slightly. The upkeep of the manse was a constant drain on my funds. I had to employ a part-time housekeeper since I was rarely in the house, to maintain its interior. She was a good-hearted soul, but she wasn't cheap. Of course, I worried when the bills came and I could not pay them. Something usually turned up. A relative in the States might decide to send me a cheque unexpectedly. I found this type of 'brinkmanship', however, very difficult to bear. Alone in the manse night after night, I often pondered my own problems and the problems of my church. In the morning, the problems would still be with me—unresolved. Perhaps it is no wonder that, as resistance to renewal became apparent within the congregation, I had to cope more and more with an increasing sense of failure.

CHAPTER SEVENTEEN

Old People

'Could you please send us a youth worker?'

It was the second time that I had put such a request to the Secretary of the Home Board. Of course, I realised that Richmond Craigmillar was already very dependant upon the Board for financial assistance. Our youth work, however, was increasing every year. It was too much of a burden for our present team to handle. Since we had not been able to locate a voluntary youth worker who was satisfactory, I had turned to the Home Board for the funds to employ a 'Professional'. The Secretary, however, was not impressed. The salary for a trained youth worker was simply not available. He suggested that we try the corporation. As I had already tried this ploy several times in the past, I rose to leave. The Secretary, however, continued to speak:

'However, I have a lay missionary who is requiring to be trained in an area such as yours. Could you use him?'

Why not?, I thought, and accepted. Any one was better than no one at all. Yet I had no notion as to how a lay missionary might be usefully employed in Niddrie.

In the event, our Lay Missionary turned out to be a sort of ecclesiastical Jack-of-all-trades. Our first man proved to be a very willing fellow, eager to take up any challenge which I might offer him. He was not, of course, a trained youth worker and he was obviously unsuited for such a role on the grounds of age, background and temperament. I suspected that, in his heart of hearts, he wanted to preach. However, we already had all the preachers we needed. Pastoral visitation as well had already been allocated to various members of the team. What was necessary, therefore, was to create some new field of endeavour for our lay missionary. For this I turned to our old people.

Until this time, our chief activity for old age pensioners had been the Guild of Friendship. Once a week they would assemble to sing choruses. Most of these were written by Moody and Sankey and had to do with blood. I found these afternoon sessions a bit depressing. Ena also took groups of women for Summer holidays in the Highlands. However, there was obviously a great deal more that needed to be done. Our church hall stood empty every afternoon until 6 p.m. Here was an opportunity! Why not create an old people's lounge, a place where elderly men and women could come for a game of dominoes or a cup of tea? Since loneliness appeared to be the greatest hazard of growing old, this would give our senior citizens an opportunity for companionship.

I put this project in the hands of our first lay missionary, Ben Mills. He made a good job of it. Taking a small room at the back of the hall, he created a homely attractive centre where pensioners might come and have a chat with one another. All sorts of games were made available. There were magazines on every table. Cups of tea and a variety of biscuits were always on hand. At first, only a half-dozen elderly ladies had the courage to come along. Soon their numbers began to swell, however. Elderly men and woman could now be seen frequently making their way slowly to the old folks' lounge. They called it their club. For many it was the only source of companionship in what otherwise would have been a solitary and lonely day.

One day I was visiting an elderly spinster in hospital. As I left the ward, I took the nurse aside.

'What is the matter with her, Sister? Do you think that she will recover?'

'There's really little wrong with her. She's suffering from malnutrition', came the reply.

I was shocked. Malnutrition was something to be found in Pakistan, not in the welfare state! When I thought about it, however, it made sense. I knew how little I liked to dine alone. Presumably, many of these single old people felt the same. Tea and a biscuit would be enough for them. Without proper nourishment, however, they would land in hospital sooner or later.

Through a conversation with a friendly town councillor, I learned about a lunch club scheme. Sponsored by the Edinburgh Corporation, it provided meals for old age pensioners at a nominal price. These meals were not intended for senior citizens who were handicapped or housebound. 'Meals on Wheels' had been created for them. Instead, this programme had been invented with solitary old people in mind. The good meal would bring them nourishment; the companionship would help to enrich their lives. The food was prepared in the large corporation cooking centres. Often it was the same menu that was given to local school children. Kept hot in large containers, the three-course meals were carried in vans to the lunch clubs which had been created to receive them.

This scheme was full of possibilities for our old people. It would be a welcome complement for our old folks' lounge. After numerous visits to interview corporation officials, I was promised that a lunch club would be allocated to our area as soon as possible. The Congregational Board was approached. With a bit of coaxing, it allowed the club to take place in the church hall. Ena organised volunteers to wait on tables and do the washing-up. We were all ready to go. No action as yet however, had been taken by the corporation. Although abundant promises had been made, they remained unfulfilled. When a letter at last arrived to tell me that there were no meals available for our old people, I was furious. I responded by return of post. In my letter, I maintained that it was scandalous that, although there were corporation lunch clubs all over Edinburgh, there was none located in Niddrie. There was a high proportion of old people in the district and every reason to brighten their lives in the midst of a difficult housing estate. The only reply that I received was silence.

One year later, an answer came. We were given permission to begin our lunch club. It would start in one month's time. We would be allocated meals for fifty old age pensioners initially on Mondays, Wednesdays and Fridays of each week. The corporation helped us to find a source of supply for the cutlery and dishes which we needed.

The letter caught us unawares. It came as a complete surprise. The team responded quickly. Ena organised the volunteers once again. David Gordon, who had succeeded Ben Mills as our lay missionary, was to work out a liaison between the new lunch club and the old folks' lounge. John and I were to serve meals as often as we could. We also volunteered to take turns transporting old people who lived in distant parts of the parish to the club.

Who should be asked to attend? Ena compiled lists of names. Some were taken from the membership of the Guild of Friendship. Others came from the senior citizens who frequented the lounge. Not all were eligible. The emphasis was upon single old people who needed good food and companionship. We wanted to make certain, as well, that there was no denominational bias in the lunch club. For this reason, we asked the district nurses to compile lists of suitable names also. From all of these sources, we compiled a membership list for the lunch club based on genuine need. However, these old people needed coaxing to come along. Some were suspicious. Others were hesitant. Some were afraid of any new venture. There was the old widow, for instance, who spent many a day weeping by herself when there was no one to hear her. She found it difficult to break away from the world of her memories and step into the world of the present. There was the elderly spinster from the Highlands who found herself allocated a house in the brutal world of Niddrie. She found it difficult to consort with people who were sometimes unclean and scarcely literate. She needed their company, all the same. The four members of our team visited every person on Ena's list. Many were shy but obviously wanting companionship. They needed a good meal as well. With a great deal of effort, we at last persuaded fifty pensioners to come along to the club.

It proved to be a great success. Soon Ena had a long waiting-list of other old people who wanted to come along. It seemed a shame to have to deny them entry but the corporation would only allow us enough meals for fifty pensioners. At first the members of the lunch club were shy with one another. That soon ended. After several weeks, they were looking forward to one another's company. Many would stay on after lunch to have a chat in the lounge. How grateful they were for the help that we gave to them. One morning I happened to meet an old blind woman as she tapped her way along the street. She was a regular member of the lunch club. Recently I had managed to acquire a second-hand wireless for her.

'How are you doin'?' I asked.

'Who is it?', she asked hesitantly.

'I'm the minister of the church'.

This time she caught my American accent.

'Oh, your Reverence. I'm so sorry I didn't know you.' With this, she knelt on the pavement and burst into tears. I struggled to get her to her feet. My face was red, but not with the cold.

'Come on now, I'll help you along for your messages.' All the way to the shops, she spoke about her gratitude. It was quite a change to have someone say, 'Thank you.'

We found our best thanks, however, in watching the lives of the old people change as they became members of the lunch club. A district nurse had given us the name of one old bachelor who lived by himself in a three-apartment house in Niddrie Mains Drive. I went to visit him. His home was indescribably filthy. The wallpaper in the sitting-room was charred as if there had been a fire recently. The old man refused my offer of the lunch club. He was all right on his own, he said. He showed me to the door. His little dog followed me down the stair, nipping my heels. I had no great personal desire to pay a return visit. The thought of the old man, however, living alone in the midst of his filthy surroundings weighed heavily upon me. As a result, John and I went back to see him. This time we did not mention the lunch club. We suggested instead that we might be able to help him to tidy up the house. The old bachelor hesitated and then reluctantly accepted. I thought that I caught sight for a moment of a gleam of gratitude beneath his scowling eyebrows.

As was so often the case, John was left to do the really nasty work. He persuaded members of the Boy Scouts to give him a hand. Together they cleaned up the old man's house. There was one room, however, that even the boys refused to touch. It was covered with excrement. It appeared that many times the dog had used the floor instead of a lamp post. John cleaned it out himself. He came back with interesting news.

'Bill', he said, 'I think that the old boy would come along to the lunch club if he could get a couple of pairs of trousers. Sometimes he can't control himself. It makes him embarrassed. That's why he's afraid to go out in company'.

We explained the problem to Ena. Resourceful as ever, she found the trousers that were needed. With his new outfit, the old man agreed to come along to the lunch club. I would collect him in my car.

'I'll give it a try', he said gruffly.

Shortly before twelve noon, I drove round the parish to pick up the lunch club members who lived far away from the church. First I collected a widow, next the Highland lady. I placed both women in the back seat. Then on I went to meet the old bachelor. When I approached his door, I was certain that he would refuse to come. No, he was ready. As his barking dog showed every readiness to go for my heels once more, I shut the door behind him quickly and helped him out to the waiting car. It was a cold day. I had the heater on and the windows closed. Slowly, I began the drive to the church. I was making small talk to the old man. Behind me, I could hear the Highland lady exclaim loudly:

'Pheuw!' she said, 'that smell!'

Hoping that my companion in the front seat had not heard her, I lowered the window slightly. We all needed a little ventilation.

'I've never smelled anything like it', she continued.

I kept up the small talk all the way to the church, speaking loudly. When we reached the hall, I helped the old folk out of the car. Then I went in to help to serve the meals. Out of the corner of my eye, I watched the old bachelor. He came in and took a seat at the table. Everyone ignored him. Everyone who came within smelling distance sat somewhere else. Finally, as the seats were filling up, an old woman sat opposite him. She was big and fat and hearty. Immediately she began to chat with him. I returned him to his house after making a previous journey with the widow and the Highland lady.

'Will you be ready on Wednesday?' I asked. To my surprise, he replied that he would. When my turn came round to collect him again, I was interested to note that he was ready and waiting outside the close. It relieved me to know that I would not have to encounter his dog again. Now he appeared to look forward to each meeting of the lunch club with anticipation. I noticed that the fat woman always sat opposite him. Once, when she was late, he kept a seat for her.

'He's got a girl friend', remarked Ena with perception.

It was true! One year later, a social worker who visited the old bachelor told John that membership in the lunch club had changed his whole attitude to life. It gave him something to look forward to with eagerness and anticipation: companionship as well as good food. That was the kind of 'thank you' which meant most to us.

The lunch club served several other purposes as well. It gave the members of our team an opportunity to chat informally with the old people. If they didn't come along to the club, something was wrong. For instance, we allowed one old couple to attend. He was very feeble; she was physically handicapped. One day they failed to appear. When Ena paid a call at the house, she found that the old man was lying dead. He had experienced a heart attack. The poor woman, unable to call for help, was lying in bed. She had been unable to lift herself and had been there for several days. The funeral took place two days later. As the couple were both Catholics, it was conducted by a local priest. The old woman needed help, however. The social work department could not find a place for her in a home immediately. The Little Sisters of Charity, whose convent was directly across the street, said that they already had more cases than they could handle adequately. So Ena visited the old woman day and night. She washed her, cleaned the house and fed her. I had never admired her dedication more than I did during these days. Several weeks later it was possible to find a place for the old woman in an old folks' home.

Catholics and Protestants attended the lunch club. Many who came, however, were indifferent to the Christian faith. Now, as they saw the volunteers and the team serving up the mashed potatoes and helping them to feel comfortable, they began to understand the nature of Christian service. As a result—without a word from any of us—a large number began to attend the Sunday morning worship service. On the behalf of all of these old age pensioners, we began to hold a flower service in the Spring of each year. It was a beautiful service of worship. Members of the Sunday School brought bouquets of flowers to the church. After worship they were distributed to the old people. Ena kept a record of those who were housebound or in hospital and bouquets were delivered to them. It was a good way to brighten the lives of the old folk and a good way to bridge the generation gap as well.

The sight of all of these old people making their way slowly toward the church day after day made a great effect upon the local community. From time to time, the sons and daughters of these pensioners would stop members of the team or members of the

Kirk Session to thank them for all that the church was doing for their parents. The old peoples' welfare organisations, once they had ceased to think that our activities rivalled their own efforts, began to co-ordinate our endeavours with their own. As for the old people themselves, they never ceased to sing the praise of all who helped with the lunch club. In the buses or at the shops, they continually voiced their gratitude. In this way, they helped others in the community to see the church as the Body of Christ which was in Niddrie to serve the needs of all who wanted help.

CHAPTER EIGHTEEN

Riot!

'There's going to be a fight at the Richmond tonight'. My informant was a young boy whom I had taken along to the swimming baths together with twelve of his pals. I asked him to tell me more.

'The Beat Group playing at the youth fellowship dance tonight is from Gilmerton', he continued, 'Our lads don't like the singer. His brother recently gave some of the Niddrie boys a "doing". Tonight they're going to show him that "Niddrie Rules the World" '.

I left the young swimmers and drove immediately back to the church, still wearing my white jersey and old Levis. Knocking on the door of the church hall, I was ushered inside by John Miller.

'None of our bouncers have turned up', John told me. 'It looks like they've been warned off. I'm expecting trouble. All day I've had anonymous phone calls promising a battle at the dance tonight. The police were informed but they advised me to go ahead with the dance. That's what we've done.'

I wished with all my heart that John had not decided to follow the policemen's advice. We had experienced difficulties with every dance we had ever presented for Niddrie young people. We had tried having dances in the church hall and at the Portobello town hall. The result was always the same: a fight. The teenager boys seemed to take it for granted that a dance was an ideal opportunity for them to demonstrate their virility in front of the lassies. The girls were every bit as bad. Often drunk on cheap wine, they would spit and claw at one another like enraged cats. I had never seen a dance which was not attended by some form of violence.

My first experience with teenage dances in Edinburgh had been at the Saint James Mission, located at the top of Leith Walk. During my early days as a divinity student, I had helped part-time at the mission. Soon I had an assignment. I was asked to make contact with teenagers in the bars and the coffee houses in order to persuade them to come to the mission dance which was held regularly on Sunday nights.

During these days I made great use of my American accent and my ignorance of the local Scottish scene. Young people seemed amused and attracted by the sound of my voice. I was given a number of informal tours of the capital city, making use of the time to gain the confidence of the teenagers who were escorting me. Soon the Teddy Boys and their girl friends began to come along to the Sunday night dances. Sometimes we had good discussions and, after every dance, there were always prayers. One Sunday night I was standing talking to a couple of lads when a tall angular boy strode across the dance floor and stopped in front of me.

'I don't like the way you look', he sneered.

'Well, go and look somewhere else', I suggested, trying to make a joke of the matter. The lad wasn't amused. In fact, he became even more enraged, taking my remark to be a reference to the fact that he was cross-eyed. In a flash, he had pulled out a long knife from beneath his jacket, while the rest of the teenagers scattered. Vainly, I looked around the dance floor, searching for other helpers. There were none in sight. I looked down at my fists. They were about to be slashed to ribbons. Suddenly, however, one of the boys stepped between us, shielding me.

'If you want to take him, you'll need to take me as well', he stated.

My cross-eyed assailant began to curse loudly and then, before I had realised quite what had taken place, he had bolted and run out the door. Good old Mike Adamson! For that was the name of the fellow who had come to my assistance. How I wished that he was with me in Niddrie now.

Of course, we had hoped that things might be different on this occasion. We had never bargained for trouble. John had asked the Congregational Board for permission to hold an all-ticket dance for the youth fellowship and their friends. By selecting the boys and girls to whom tickets were to be sold, he had hoped that it might be possible to avoid violence. As soon as I stepped into the crowded hall, however, I knew that this had been a false hope. The young people were waiting for trouble. Over one hundred and fifty teenagers were there, mostly school-children. They were dancing to the ear-splitting sounds of the Beat Group or loitering in the dark corners smoking. There was a tension in the air which was not the result of the music. Most were expecting a battle.

Closing-time for the local pubs was rapidly

approaching, the most difficult hour in a difficult evening. I stationed myself inside the hall, close enough to the rear exit to be certain that it was kept fastened against entry. John stood bravely by the front door. There he patiently explained to the groups of lads who arrived without tickets that they would not be allowed to enter the dance. The boys argued; some threatened. John held the door.

About this time, two of the bouncers finally arrived, leaders from the local adventure playground. I was happy to see them. I asked one to relieve me at my post at the rear of the hall. As I walked across the dance floor, I saw the other bouncer open the front door slightly. Immediately it swung open and a gang of youths fell upon him, throwing him to the floor. Others rushed into the hall. As I went to the aid of the stricken man, John stopped the rest from further entry. To my surprise and relief, as I approached, the boys jumped away from the bouncer. I raised him to his feet. He was dazed and bleeding. I helped him to find a seat. John meanwhile was rounding up the rest of the gate-crashers. He forced them to leave. As the Beat Group continued to play, the boys and girls began to dance once again. I went outside to have a look around. I could only see scattered groups of youngsters. As a result, I concluded that we had experienced our quota of violence for the evening and since order had been restored to the hall, I decided to return to the manse. On the way home, I stopped by the local police station and asked that a man be sent along to the church hall to keep an eye on the situation. No one could come immediately I was told, because the men were 'between shifts'. There would be help later. Although I was uneasy, I returned to my home.

As it turned out, the affair was far from finished. Shortly after my departure, a group of thirty youths assembled near the church. Many were drunk. They had been told that the hall was full of 'outsiders' from Gilmerton. They could not see for themselves if the report was true. Lacking tickets, they could not gain entry. Drink gave them the courage that they needed. They decided to try to force the door. John held it firmly closed. Nearby residents now telephoned for the police. Although patrolmen had driven by the church at intervals, none were to be seen now that the crowd seemed truly to be out of hand. At last a panda car drove up just as the crowd of boys—now seventy-five in number—made a determined assault on the hall door. After calling for help, the two policemen left their vehicle. With their backs against the door, they warded off attacks. They were struck by iron railings torn from nearby fences and bruised by stones and other missiles thrown by the youths. While they held their ground, the mob surrounded their car and overturned it.

Inside the hall, there was general consternation. The Beat Group continued to play. Few were dancing, however. Most of the youngsters were eating crisps or drinking fruit-juice. Some of the bolder ones wanted to go outside to view the battle. John kept them in. The sole topic of conversation was the disturbance. One girl decided at this time to visit the ladies' room. A moment later, she emerged screaming, closely followed by two invading youths. Having ripped off the iron gate on the window, the boys had broken the glass and gained entry. They strode into the hall ready to fight. The more they looked around, the more bewildered they became. They could not locate any of the offending 'outsiders' from Gilmerton. Instead, they recognised almost every young face. Shaking their heads, they left the hall peacefully. It was too late, however, for them to communicate their news to the crowd which had assembled outside.

The police had now arrived in force. Five more panda cars had been added to the one which now lay toppled over on its side in the street. As they converged on the youths, a voice from the mob shouted:

'If we can't get the Gilmerton boys, we'll get the police.'

A pitched battle ensued. Matched against the policemen were some six dozen lads armed with improvised weapons. For several minutes the battle raged. Then the boys broke and ran, scattering into small groups to various parts of the housing estate. The police pursued them. Some of the youngsters sought sanctuary in the homes of friends. Others hid in darkened gardens. A few found safety before their own firesides. In the end, however, most of the leaders were apprehended. Many of these boys had been recognised by the police during the course of the battle. They waited silently for them to return home or to make an appearance at the local fish and chip shop. One boy, ambushed in this fashion, suddenly found himself the victim of five police truncheons. His friends later claimed police brutality. Patrol cars were being filled with youths, many of whom simply opened the opposite door and slipped away into the night. Others, less fortunate, were taken away to jail. By the end of the evening, thirteen lads were waiting to appear before the magistrate.

During the whole of the battle, John had stead-fastly refused to allow any of the dancers to leave the hall. He did not want them to be involved in the violence. Now he released his hold on the front door. Immediately, the hall was filled with anxious parents. They had stood outside watching the violence. Only three, however, had gone to the aid of the police. Some took their children from the hall immediately. Others were content with the assurance that their children had not been injured. The Beat Group continued to play! No one, however, was listening. Conversation centred on the battle which had taken place. Already, myths were being manufactured. Coats were now gathered and gradually the hall emptied. The group played the last dance. John and his volunteers began to sweep the floor. The evening was over.

At two o'clock in the morning, we held an impromptu conference at the manse. Present with me were John, John's wife Mary, who had calmly been dispensing orange juice and crisps during the height of the battle, and a member of the youth fellowship who had missed the last bus home. Huddled around the electric fire, we discussed all that had taken place.

I was worried. What effect would the affair have upon the youth work of the church? We had ex-perienced fighting at previous dances, but nothing like this. A newspaper reporter, by bad luck, had been present as well! Undoubtedly, therefore, the violence at the church hall would be reflected in the morning headlines. What would Niddrie people, always so sensitive about adverse publicity, think about all that had taken place? What would be the reaction of the congregation which had often lost patience with our efforts to reach the young people of the area?

John was more serene. He pointed out that little of the violence had actually occurred within the church hall. Moreover, no one from the youth fellowship—or their friends—had actually been injured. There were a few indications that the youths had not been hostile to the church or to the members of the team. A few of the invaders had actually left the hall when John spoke to them. Others, whom many might have called 'animals', were still sensible enough to take the violence out of the building and into the street. Suddenly John groaned. He had suddenly remembered that three of the boys taken away in the police van were members of his football team. He had only twelve hours to find replacements!

On the following day, several facts emerged. The thirteen boys 'lifted' by the police were duly charged and detained without bail until they could make their plea. Officially the matter was one of public order. The church was not involved. Yet local opinion believed that the church was very much involved in the whole affair. Many saw it as a public disgrace for the whole community. According to three old age pensioners chatting at a local shop, Richmond Craigmillar was at fault. Too much was being done for the young people. It could only lead to trouble. By-standers at the battle, however, had been heard to remark that it was a shame that the church could not be allowed to hold a dance for young people without the risk of violence. Why did every activity undertaken for local youngsters have to end in a brawl? It was the conclusion that only a few 'bad yins' were to blame. Seventy-five, however, seemed to me to be quite a few.

When John reported the damage to the hall convener on the following Sunday morning—a broken window, damaged iron grill, a few minor repairs—he was met with an attitude of indignation mixed with resignation: 'You're only here for twelve more months. In twenty years, Niddrie has swallowed up twenty mugs like you.'

On the whole, however, the incident passed with little comment from the people who attended the Sunday morning worship service at the church. I gave a brief statement about the affair from the pulpit. Reactions indicated indifference. A few people even indicated that such difficulties were 'occupational hazards' for any one who wanted to help the people who were resident in the district.

Our youth work appeared to be completely unaffected by what had taken place. My own football team was typical. I had taken over as manager after a former secretary had absconded with the club funds. Many of my team members had younger brothers who had been 'lifted' because of the disturbance.

'They're mugs anyway', said one fellow.

'Fools', said another.

I was delighted by this response. Many of my players had previously 'done time'. They gave no indication, however, that they wanted to be drawn into further violence because of the incident at the dance. Disgust was their typical reaction.

On the next Wednesday evening, I received a delegation at my vestry. It was composed of the parents of the thirteen boys who had been 'lifted'. One mother explained why they had come...

'Will you go up to court and speak for the boys?' she asked.

In my own heart, I was not sure that Christian charity should extend this far. Fortunately, I didn't have to make a decision. It had been made for me. I had not been present during the battle when the boys had been arrested. When I explained my position the mother persevered:

'Will you at least go up and visit the lads?'

I agreed to do so. The next morning I went from cell to cell at Saughton Prison talking with the youngsters. I knew them all. They were a pathetic sight. All of them were still dressed in the clothes in which they had been 'lifted'. A few faces displayed cuts, scratches and bruises. All maintained innocence:

'I didn't do nothin!'

'I wasn't there', and so on.

It soon became apparent, however, that every effort was being made on the part of the Prosecution to teach the boys a lesson. When all pled 'Not Guilty', the case was sent up to the High Court. Trial was fixed for February, 1969. All of the boys were given the opportunity for bail. During the intervening months, some of the youngsters continued to protest their innocence. Others left this task to the lawyers who had been hired on their behalf. One night, I was walking past the 'Chippie' when a member of 'the thirteen' came across to speak to me:

'I've had a list of the prosecution witnesses',

he said, 'There's a minister against us. Is that you?'

The minister in question was John Miller. He had been summoned against his will to speak on behalf of the Prosecution. Several days later, I received a telephone call from the counsel for the defence. Would I appear as a witness on behalf of 'The Thirteen'? I protested that I had not been present when the incident occurred. My protest went unheeded. The next morning's post brought a subpoena to appear at the High Court.

And so the trial began. On the first day the charges against nine of the boys were dropped. There was insufficient evidence. I wondered privately how the case could ever have reached the High Court in the first place. Weighing his words carefully, John gave his evidence. A packed court listened. Within the crowd sat the nine boys who had been freed, together with many other teenagers. They chewed gum, giggled and gossiped with one another as the trial continued. Although John's evidence was ultimately favourable to the boys, it is doubtful that many in the court understood its 'bias'. It was enough for them that he had been called to testify by the Prosecution. As for me, my testimony, useless as it would have been, was never given. The remaining boys were eventually found 'Guilty'. Two were admonished. The other two were each sentenced for one year's imprisonment.

As we feared, the matter had been fully covered by the Press. During the trial, it was featured in the headlines of the *Edinburgh Evening News*:

'DRAWN BATONS' ORDER AS 60 ATTACK
NINE YOUTHS ARE CLEARED AT MOB TRIAL
MOB RIOT: TWO GO TO CELLS AS WOMEN WEEP

Because of all of this attention, the plight of the boys drew a great deal of attention on the street corners and in the public houses of Niddrie. There was general jubilation when the verdict was made public. The nine boys who had escaped punishment celebrated in parties which lasted into the wee hours of the morning. All the same, it was noticed in future months that they were seldom to be seen at local dances or hanging about the front of the chip shop looking for trouble. Perhaps the police had succeeded. Perhaps the boys had learned their lesson after all.

The police, however, obviously wished to teach the church a lesson as well. In many ways, the members of the team were made aware that local constables did not approve of our efforts to help young people. John received several lectures from police officers. One morning, as I was driving a lad in search of a job, I was pulled up by a panda car. I stepped out immediately, dressed in clerical costume. I asked what was the matter. I knew that I had not been speeding. Was there some difficulty about my car? One of the policemen eyed me up and down:

'Where are you the minister?' he asked.

'Richmond Craigmillar, the Church along the road', I replied. There was silence. 'But what is the matter?' I asked. The policemen looked at me.

'We just don't like the company you keep', he said, nodding at the car.

'Surely you don't mean the boy. I'm taking him to get a job', I exclaimed.

'That's right', he added.

Getting back into the panda car, the police drove

off, and I was left standing, meditating on the possibility that Scotland might become a police state.

CHAPTER NINETEEN

One Way to Go

My study was still cold from the previous night's frost as I took my seat at my desk. It was eight a.m. and my morning cup of coffee had not yet jolted me into life. At that moment, the telephone rang. It was a woman—a leader in a church organisation—she was beside herself with anger. For twenty minutes she tore into me. At the end of her monologue, she declared that she was resigning. I was bewildered and confused. I could not piece together the reason for her attack. As I thought about her words over my second cup of coffee, it became apparent that her daughter, a leader of a children's youth club, had reported a complaint to her mother. Normally the youngsters had the use of the church hall. However, on the preceding evening, the social committee had asked them to make a concession and to conduct their activities in a back room. The hall was needed in order to decorate for a 'cafe continental' which was due to be held there on the next night. I was being blamed, since both mother and daughter believed that I had given the committee the permission to take this step. Was I truly guilty of this unforgivable crime? I searched my memory. It was full of lots of things: old folks, interviews, youth clubs, etc. Yet I could not recall having said anything special to the convener of the social committee. The whole affair, of course, only disguised the determination of some of our older members that no-one should yield before the onslaught of new ideas. If the members of the old regime could do nothing else, they could at least inflict the maximum amount of pain by the process of resignation.

This dispute caught me off guard. I was pierced by the bitterness of the woman's tongue. In former days, I might have dealt with the matter in an objective fashion, considering the pros and cons of the lady's resignation, I might have been able to see the problem in perspective. Perhaps the Church would be well rid of her! I was not able to do so, however. Spiritually and physically, I was exhausted. The good woman and others like her were fighting to retain their position in the church. For them, it was a desperate fight, a fight for their lives. Without their status in the congregation, they were nothing. No doubt, however, they had altered the very nature of the church. In their view, the church had not been created to bring the good news of Jesus Christ to others in the parish. Instead, it had been created to sustain their own inadequate lives. At one time I might have tried to sympathise with their position and to understand it, although persevering with the call to mission. Now, however, that was no longer possible. I was bankrupt, defenceless. The acrimony of the woman's words easily upset me. Deeply wounded by such party strife, I took advantage of a scheduled trip to Aberdeen as an opportunity for prayer and meditation.

In the silence of my hotel room, I pondered my own future in the Christian church. Of course, I admitted that there were fights and squabbles in any social activity or organisation. What defeated me was that the same sort of problems should arise within the church, the Body of Christ. Here were men and women who professed to believe in Jesus Christ. On the other hand, they often descended to a type of gutter-politics which would have made the members of a social club or a community organisation ashamed of themselves. Although the words and deeds were perhaps more brutal at Richmond Craigmillar, I had gained the impression over the years that members of other churches behaved in a similar fashion. No wonder that many good men and women simply shrugged their shoulders and kept well clear! I felt a temptation to do the same. I had been called by Christ to serve others in his name. All the same, it often appeared that my ministry was simply to smooth over a succession of endless bickerings between rival factions in the congregation.

I was equally aware that my spiritual life had suffered. I no longer had the solace and comfort of private prayer. I prayed during the day, of course—a continuous chain of 'professional' prayers, in weddings and funerals, prayers which most often were indifferently received and seldom seemed to be shared by my fellow worshippers. At the end of such days, I had little strength to shape my own personal prayers to God. Many times, with a mumbled plea for help, I would simply tumble into bed. I needed that help badly now.

It was the custom that a resignation from a church leader should be forwarded to the Kirk Session for consideration. One morning after morning worship, the elders met together. Most of the discussion took the form of an attack upon the team. Since we were so seldom in the church, we could not possibly be aware of what took place in the building. One elder suggested that a committee be formed to investigate the activities undertaken by the team members. How did each member spend each working-day? Up until this point, I had taken no part in the debate. However, as tempers began to explode, I intervened. Surely, I suggested, differences between church organisations should not involve the Kirk Session in such heated arguments.

'The only reason we are members of the church is because each of us believes in Jesus Christ. Remembering his teachings, we ought to attempt to understand and to forgive one another.' I explained.

'I've never listened to such rubbish', replied one elder. The rest nodded in agreement. In that meeting, they began to destroy my hopes for the future of Richmond Craigmillar.

The whole affair quickly quieted down, however. The woman who had submitted her resignation withdrew it when she was approached by a delegation from the Session. Flattered by all the commotion which she had caused, she said that she could forgive me. Anyhow, she had subsequently learned that I had never been guilty of the misdemeanor in the first place!

I was left severely shaken. When I reviewed the years of my ministry in Niddrie, I found that my faith was stronger than ever. More and more, however, I found that it was difficult to reconcile this faith with the structures of the church. It was not simply that some of these structures were out-of-date and laughable. More than that, some aspects of church life seemed positively harmful and destructive to faith. The eldership, for instance, had originally been intended to be an extension of the pastoral ministry in the church. However, it could easily be turned round and used to bolster petty egos and arrogant ambitions. Church activities and organisations could wreck considerable damage through internecine warfare. When people who believed in God were being turned away from the church because of internal strife and petty bickering, then it was reasonable for me to consider whether I could not best follow my call for serve Jesus Christ within some other context or institution. I considered the possibility of re-training and even wrote to Harvard University to apply for admission to the School of Education. When a letter came in response to tell me that I would need to sit several entrance examinations, I put the possibility firmly out of my mind.

However, despite my inward doubts, the problems of the church continued. One of its major difficulties was its financial need. Every year of my ministry had seen an increase of approximately two hundred pounds in the total giving. However, with rising costs, this only meant that we were breaking-even. We had made little progress toward the assumption of financial independence from the Home Board. An assessment of the figures from the previous year revealed that our free-will offering scheme had only increased by five pounds. Our net increase was due, ironically enough, to the competition between the 'old guard' and the new social committee to demonstrate which faction could raise the greatest amount. of money.

After considering our difficulties, it occurred to me that the major premise underlying the various financial schemes of the Church of Scotland was that a member must attend a worship service in order to give. In our own congregation, many members who might have wished to attend were prevented from doing that. Family and business obligation intervened. The result was that the offering plate was often half-empty, particularly since many worshippers did not bring along their FWO envelopes for Sundays when they failed to appear. In fact, our church was chiefly being supported by old age pensioners. Something had to be done.

One Friday evening, I was paying a pastoral call on one of the well-known leaders of the congregation. There was a knock at the door. It was the man who had come to collect her insurance money. Five minutes later, there was a second knock. This was the man who visited her regularly to collect her pools' contributions. While they chatted at the door, it occurred to me that this was the type of collection which was familiar to most of the people in the parish. Friday night was collection night. The woman of the house stayed in to disperse the funds. Why not, therefore, organise a collection scheme from the church on the same basis? If all the church members could be approached in this manner once a week on a Friday night, we might even be able to dispense with the offering plate at the morning worship service!

I presented this idea to the Congregational Board. I added that, if this notion failed to gain acceptance, some other solution to our financial problems would have to be found. My scheme did not prove popular, however. Many members of the Board felt that it would be embarrassing to pay calls on neighbours and friends, members of the church, asking for money on a Friday night. Anyhow, they had to stay in themselves to pay the pools and the insurance money! All the same, the Board failed to present any other constructive alternative to the scheme. It did decide, however, that the free-will offering scheme should be emphasised once again to the members of the church. Visitors should be asked to take the envelopes round to all of the people in the congregation, explaining our financial difficulties. The Board asked for volunteers for this project. One hundred and forty invitations were issued for a special meeting: eighty to prospective volunteers, sixty to Board members. In the event, fifteen people appeared at the meeting. Since there were not enough people to proceed with the scheme, an appeal was launched from the pulpit and the envelopes were at last delivered. Most were simply pushed through members' letter-boxes. For several months the average weekly offering increased by five pounds. Then, as apathy increased and the Summer months approached, the money in the offering plate began to dwindle once more.

Financially, we had failed to get the church off the ground. I still had hopes, however, that we might be able to alter the actual church building and the social s.... .tures of our congregation. To this end, I posted ....ving letter to the Members of the Kirk

....rch always seems to be

involved in a battle for survival. Recently, mounting costs together with poor congregations have made the problem still more acute. I know that you must worry and wonder what our future must be and I can assure you that I spend a good deal of time thinking about the same problem. For this reason, I am placing a number of proposals before you. I do not know if they contain the answers to our difficulties but perhaps we could find the answers by debating them together.

First of all, I would propose that we invite a team of architects to survey the present suite of buildings with a view to converting them into a chapel (seating 100—500) and a larger suite of halls. Such work, if agreed upon, would need the permission of the Presbytery and I would propose that we request a grant to cover the cost.

With a small chapel and a large suite of halls, I would propose the following changes:

(1) Communion once a month. No communion cards necessary. Communion open to all members.

(2) Baptism and marriages only for those people who are already church members.

(3) Abolition of elders' districts. Visitation of the sick and housebound only.

(4) Appointment of a full-time caretaker for the suite of buildings. The Congregational Board to levy a charge on each organisation using the buildings to cover his salary and the cost of maintenance. That charge (a donation) to vary according to the ability of the specific organisation to meet it.

I am sending these proposals to you in order to provide you with ample time for consideration. I know that you will respect the fact that this is Session business and, as such, that it be treated in private. I would propose that we meet together on Wednesday, April 16, 1969 at 7.30 p.m. in order to hold our discussion.

With best wishes,

Sincerely,
W. J. CHRISTMAN

These proposals were intended to strengthen the congregation spiritually. They aimed at underlining the significance of the worship service and the sacraments. By liberating the elders from some obligations for visitation, I hoped to be able to give them a greater part in the missionary activities of the church.

One morning, however, after a sleepless night due to an attack of 'flu, I heard the postman's knock. I staggered down the stairs to see what he had brought. I received a shock. I had been awarded a Fellowship to Harvard University, with the most substantial grant possible. I was asked to begin my studies in June. Evidently, although I had not persevered with my application, my initial letter had begun the process which ended with the acceptance in my hand. Here was a rare opportunity! I had considered the possibility of re-training. With this Fellowship, I could do it. There was a possibility that, at the end of my studies, I could teach in the United States. Over a cup of tea the next night, I discussed the matter with my mentor, Professor Cheyne. He advised me to remain at Richmond

Craigmillar for at least another year. There was wisdom in his advice. It was traditional in the Church of Scotland for a minister to remain in his first Charge for at least five years. I had been there for four only. But what if I didn't want to remain within the institutional church at all? The prospect of twelve more months in Niddrie depressed me thoroughly. I had few hopes or illusions left. Believing deeply in Jesus Christ, I was more and more convinced that I could not continue to believe within the context of the church.

As I entered the manse, the telephone was ringing. It was the Depute Director of the Home Board. He wanted to read to me an article which was due to appear in a Home Mission Bulletin. It was an article about our team. I listened closely as he read. Phrases stuck in my mind: 'On the face of it, it's a failure as a kirk . . . a write-off church in a write-off area . . . .'

The author described me as 'a fast-talking American' and an ecclesiastical 'loner'. When the reader finished, I was filled with anger mixed with despair. Was that all we were worth to the Church of Scotland? It was a cheap article written by a man who criticised us a bit, ridiculed us a bit and emphasised all the odd things that the team was forced to do in order to bring the gospel of Jesus Christ to the people of the parish. When I protested strongly, I was told that it was already too late. I could, however, add one final sentence to the completed article. I did: 'The minister maintains firmly that the sole justification for the presence of his team and the church in Craigmillar is to proclaim the gospel of Jesus Christ in word and action.'

To proclaim the Gospel! If however, the local congregation persisted in defying the claims of that gospel and if the official line of the Church of Scotland was to snigger rather than to support us in our efforts, was it not all for nothing? Or, if not for nothing, would I not better serve Christ Jesus in some other sphere? That night I made up my mind. I would go to Harvard. I postponed the announcement of my decision, however, until after the next Kirk Session meeting. If my proposals were treated seriously by the elders—if there was any glimmer of hope for the church—then I would gladly continue at Richmond Craigmillar.

When the elders met, I began by explaining the reasons for making the proposals which had been posted to them. So violent was the reaction that I had to call for order to be allowed to finish speaking. Opinion was wholeheartedly against innovation. One man proceeded to express his disapproval of my entire ministry. He maintained that I had lead the church in the wrong direction since the moment of my induction. In his opinion, I had not answered the questions of the vacancy committee honestly. It was apparent that the church had subsequently suffered through lack of attention from its minister. Its members needed to be visited. If visited, they would come again to the church. Money would flow in to the offering once more. It was obvious that he was completely disillusioned with my ministry. Had the vacancy committee been meeting again, he would have sought a more suitable candidate to lead their church. I kept silent as several other elders spoke supporting his position. No-one dissented from the opinions that were being expressed. At last

I intervened and attempted to remind the elders that the church was virtually kept alive through the generosity of the Home Board for the purpose of mission. At the point, several elders became quite angry. This was their church, they said. No-one could tell them how best to minister to the needs of their own congregation. The meeting was adjourned.

I could not find it in my heart to be angry with the elders. Frustrated in their day-to-day lives, they found it difficult to leave their frustrations behind when they came to church. All the same, I could not overlook the deep discontentment which lay behind their expressions of anger. They were no longer able to support the general direction of my ministry. I had lost their confidence. Although I was willing to admit that I had made all sorts of mistakes, however, I was still not willing to admit that the course which I had followed was the wrong one. Looking back, I could see no other course which I could possibly have followed. To do otherwise was the denial of my call and my faith.

'You will make me a hypocrite', I had cried out at one point in the Session meeting as the elders had put forward the impossible demands of a petty congregation.

This did not dissuade them: 'Every man has to learn to do certain things which he does not like in order to keep his job', was their retort.

There had been plenty of things which I had not liked about my job at Craigmillar. I had endured every one, however, because I believed in the direction which the team was following. It was the way of cross-bearing. It was the way of Christ Jesus. To turn my back on all those people who needed to hear the gospel of Jesus Christ in order to satisfy the demands made by petty politics in a bickering congregation appeared to me to be soul-destroying.

Writing to Harvard that night, I accepted the Fellowship. Several weeks later, with the permission of the Presbytery, I was on my way. I hoped that it was also the way of Jesus Christ.

CHAPTER TWENTY

Home-coming

The telephone rang, shattering my slumber. As I groped about the darkened room struggling to find it, my eyes sought out the face of my alarm clock. It was four in the morning. The operator told me that there was a call from Scotland and soon I was talking with the interim moderator of Lochwood Parish Church in the large housing estate of Easterhouse in Glasgow. He told me that the church was considering me as a candidate for the vacant pulpit. Members of the vacancy committee had been impressed by a tape recording of one of my sermons which Ena Finlayson had sent them of one of our Christmas Eve services in Niddrie. If the committee did decide to call me, could I come at once? I hesitated, and then replied in the affirmative. After all, remembering the chaos of those Christmas Eve services, it seemed possible that the vacancy committee in Easterhouse might well have second thoughts about my ability to preach! The good people of Lochwood might just as easily decide not to call me at all.

When I replaced the receiver, I sat back and thought over the events which had taken place during the six months since I had left Scotland. These had been months of healing for me. At the beginning, my sleep had been plagued by memories of Niddrie. Over and over again, I thought about what I should have done or might have done. So I tossed and turned through each uneasy night.

But, as the time passed, I felt myself being restored. I told no one that I had been a minister. That didn't matter. No-one asked any questions in the first place. The students that I met were friendly and cordial. They accepted me, and that acceptance was balm to my injured spirit. My classes in education were interesting and I made use of my options to study sociology. I longed to learn the answers to the questions which still haunted me about Richmond Craigmillar. And I began to find a few.

As my exhaustion passed away, my interior life of prayer increased. Inevitably I found myself wanting to attend church again, to share the faith of others who wanted to follow Jesus Christ, to participate in the worship of God.

Here then was a direct challenge by telephone from Scotland. But did I want to accept it? In five months' time I would have received my degree at Harvard and would be able to teach anywhere in the United States. The people here had been so kind to me. Did I really want to go back to a situation which would be every bit as demanding as the one which I had faced in Niddrie?

They telephoned a second time. The Call was given; I accepted. And, as soon as I had made my travel arrangements, I was on my way back to Scotland. Before I left, I wrote the following letter to one of the church elders who had shared my ministry with me in Richmond Craigmillar:

January 24, 1970

Dear Arthur,

I've been thinking a lot about you this morning
so I've decided to write to you.

During the last month I've had a couple of phone
calls from Scotland and the long and short of it is that
I've been asked to preach as Sole Nominee for Lochwood
East Church in Easterhouse. And I've decided to accept,
even though it means giving up my studies at Harvard
in order to do it.

I guess the feeling which has bothered me most
about leaving Niddrie is the notion that I had let you down.
In accepting this job, I've been thinking a lot about you
because I don't want to let any more Arthur Gillieses down.
When I came to Niddrie just out of college, I had a beautiful
idea of what a Church could be. Four years later, I was
shocked and disillusioned by what Richmond Craigmillar
really was. Even after excuses have been made for my
health, that was why I really left. I just couldn't
understand; I just couldn't take it.

During the months that I have been here, most of my
research and reading has been trying to find out what
makes a place like Niddrie the kind of place it is--and
what makes Richmond Craigmillar the kind of place it is.
Now that I think I understand these things, I am ready
to go and serve in a similar type of Church. My idealistic
notion of the Church is gone. But I still think realistically
that the Church can be useful in caring for some people
in a difficult situation. That is why I am going back.
I am not writing to apologise, therefore--that would just
be apologising for being a human being. But I am writing
because I feel that I owe it to you--and to myself--not
to let down any more Arthur Gillieses.

I should be back in a couple of weeks. I know that
I'll be busy with getting things arranged but I would like
to come out and see you and the family. Of course, I'm broke.
But we'll manage. Things always seem to work out. Yesterday
I had a phone call from a couple of my college friends.
Without my knowing, a couple of them had gone together and
put up the money for my flight back to Scotland. I guess
that was one of the nicest gifts I've ever had--and they
don't have much money either.

Anyhow, all the best.

Sincerely,

Bill Christman

I never posted that letter. Perhaps because I had really written it for myself. But from time to time during the next seven years of my ministry in Easterhouse, I would take it out and read it over again. Even now, as minister of Lansdowne Parish Church in Glasgow, I find it helpful to look at it every now and then. I was married in 1975 and, in the same year, became a naturalised British citizen. As a result, my American citizenship was revoked. When the American Consul in Edinburgh summoned me in order to cancel my passport, he said:

'I hope you realise what you're doing. You're cutting the umbilical cord.'

Perhaps he was right. But there are times when I have had cause to wonder. Several days ago, a well-meaning matron crossed to where I was standing at a wedding reception. Having listened to me speak for a few moments, she put on her most gracious smile and asked:

'Are you enjoying your holiday over here?'

It's been some holiday!